LOST
BUILDINGS OF
BIRMINGHAM

LOST
BUILDINGS OF
BIRMINGHAM

ROY THORNTON

THE HISTORY PRESS

First published in the United Kingdom in 2009 by
The History Press · The Mill
Brimscombe Port · Stroud · Gloucestershire · GL5 2QG

British Library Cataloguing in Publication Data
A catalogue record for this book is available from the British Library.

ISBN 978-07509-5099-2

Typeset in 10.5/13pt Galliard.
Typesetting and origination by
The History Press
Printed and bound in England.

Contents

Introduction

The idea for this book came within a few weeks of starting another book, *Victorian Buildings of Birmingham*, as I came to realise more clearly how many Victorian buildings had been demolished, particularly since the end of the Second World War. It also followed that many buildings had been lost to allow the Victorian buildings to be erected, although in most cases these had been more modest in scale and details of them had not been recorded. However, there were exceptions.

For a building to be covered in this book it must have been demolished and the Birmingham City Library Service must have an illustration of it which is suitable to be used. The collection is very extensive, but some desirable examples have had to be excluded because I could not find what I wanted, which may be my fault.

A good proportion of the selected buildings are in or close to the city centre and so I have decided to start with these and concentrate afterwards on specific building types. Where city centre buildings belong to one of these specific categories I have dealt with them, for the most part, in their category.

As there will be a photograph of every building, I have decided not to include descriptions of them and have provided information of this kind very sparingly, thus allowing more buildings to be included.

Some of the examples were lost before any of us were born and can provide information and interest only. However, there are many that have been lost in the lifetime of those who are older and, hopefully, for them there will be fond memories.

Acknowledgements

All of the photographs in the book, with the exception of five, have been taken from the collection of Archives and Heritage, Birmingham Central Library and the copyright for these photographs remains with the library. They may not be reproduced without the express permission of the library. The other five photographs, which are acknowledged where shown, have been supplied by the Reference Section of the Sutton Coldfield Library and the same restrictions with copyright and reproduction applies with these photographs.

I should like to express my thanks to Patrick Baird and all the staff of the Local Studies and History Section (now part of Archives and Heritage) of Birmingham Central Library and to Marian Baxter and all the staff of the Reference Section of Sutton Coldfield Library for the help they have given to me in such a patient and friendly way.

Finally, I should like to thank my editor, Michelle Tilling, for the support and encouragement she has given to me at all times.

ONE

City Centre

CORPORATION STREET

All of the original buildings of Corporation Street, between New Street and Steelhouse Lane, were designed within a single generation. The first building application was submitted in April 1879 and the last in June 1900; both of these buildings are still standing. Any date I show in relation to a building will refer to the year of the application and not to its completion.

I referred to Corporation Street in some detail in *Victorian Buildings of Birmingham* and, consequently, shall not go through the preambles again. Suffice to say that the area acquired to enable the street to be built contained some of the worst buildings in the town and over 13,000 people were displaced and had to find new living accommodation as, at that time, the council was not empowered to build houses.

I intend to list all of the illustrated demolished buildings in sequence starting from New Street and go along the west (left hand) side to the last building to be demolished on the far side of the Old Square, and then cross the road and return to New Street starting at 150–8, which was occupied by the Birmingham Household Supply Association. I should mention that there was a group of eight buildings further down the east side, between Ryder Street and Aston Street, that have been demolished, and for which I have found no photographs.

The first building I shall mention was between Cherry Street and Bull Street:

North-Western Arcade. This building of 1882, designed by William Jenkins, was best known as North-Western Arcade. It ran through to Temple Row and there is still an arcade in the same location. The firm of Wilkinson & Riddell was the owner and main occupier, and the offices on the upper floors were known, appropriately enough, as Arcade Chambers. It was an attractive stone, Renaissance-style building, craving for symmetry but foiled by the constraints of the site.

North-Western Arcade, 1900.

Westminster Chambers.

This building, on the near corner of Bull Street, known as **Westminster Chambers**, was owned by William Ross and the application was made by William Ross Jnr. in 1882. The only people I have discovered with those names are a plasterer named William Ross and a builder and contractor named William Ross Jnr. operating in Small Heath. The building was one of the least distinguished in Corporation Street and might have been designed by the applicant, but if it was designed by an architect the only clue I can offer is that William Ross owned two other buildings in Corporation Street, both of which were designed by Dempster & Heaton.

The original building for **Lewis's** was built on the far corner of Bull Street in 1885 and was designed by Yeoville Thomason. Joseph Chamberlain had invited David Lewis, who owned stores in the north of England, to open a similar one in Birmingham and, after investigating, he decided that this was the best position.

Lewis's.

I cannot say whether it was the most important shop in Birmingham in its early days, but it was in my younger days and, in common with countless others, I spent many hours in the original building's successor, built in the early 1920s and which still remains, albeit not as Lewis's.

Berlin House was on the corner of Old Square and stretched back to the Minories. The 1882 application was made by Kirk & Jones and the shop premises were occupied by Jevons & Mellor, Hosier. The building was demolished in the early 1920s to allow for the erection of the first phase of the new building for Lewis's, which was built while the original store remained.

131–51 Corporation Street. This site was the subject of an ambitious application made in 1890 for an exhibition hall, hotel and three shops, made by J.P. Sharp & Co. *Kelly's Directory* of 1892 refers to the Birmingham Exhibition Hall, Winter Gardens & County Hotel Ltd., but, by 1896 this had become County Buildings and Wesleyan & General Assurance Society and, in addition, there were several shops.

Berlin House.

131–51 Corporation Street.

The proposed interior of the exhibition hall.

In 1895 Ewen Harper submitted an application for alterations on behalf of the society which had become the owners of the property. Later the society moved to new premises in Steelhouse Lane, designed by Harper. For many years, before it was demolished, the building bore a large sign proclaiming 'Crane's Pianos'.

It is time to cross the road, remembering first to look both ways.

150–8 Corporation Street. The owner and occupier of this building which dates from 1880 (one of the earliest in Corporation Street) for most of its existence was the Birmingham Household Supply Association Ltd. In its last years the shop premises were occupied by Maple's the Furnishers.

The building was designed by Martin & Chamberlain, one of four built by the practice. Unfortunately none of them survive.

150–8 Corporation Street.

126–30 Corporation Street.

126–30 Corporation Street. This building of 1886 was designed by F.B. Osborn & Reading on behalf of the Trustees of Central Hall and replaced the Methodist Church in Cherry Street. After a few years it was found to be inadequate for its purpose and Central Hall was built to replace it at 196–224 Corporation Street at the turn of the century.

By 1907 the building was being used to show vaudeville entertainment and its use changed in 1911 when it became a cinema, a function which continued until 1932. The building was known as King's Hall even when the cinema was called Royal Cinema De Luxe.

After the cinema closed, the building became a market and this powerful Gothic-style brick building was disfigured by the signs advertising 'King's Hall Market'. The building, as with the others in the vicinity, was demolished in the early 1960s.

104–8 Corporation Street. These premises were owned by Central Buildings Co. Ltd. and W. Hubard made the application for the building in 1886. In the early years the upper floors were occupied by the Central Club and it was referred to

104–8 Corporation Street.

in the application, but later it became a YWCA hostel. It was an attractive four-storey Renaissance-style building.

90–102 Corporation Street. This building on the corner of Bull Street was erected for A.R. Dean, House Furnisher, in 1885 and the architect was William Jenkins. The office section was called Dalton House and Dean's occupied the shop premises, nos 90–8. Later tenants included Halford and Dunn, the tailors. Assuming this perspective is correct, this building must have had the biggest proportion of glazing to solid wall of any of the original buildings in Corporation Street and yet I cannot remember noticing anything significant about it.

90–102 Corporation Street.

74–8 Corporation Street. In 1824 John Cadbury set up as a tea and coffee dealer at 93 Bull Street and, from 1835, started making cocoa and chocolate, firstly at Crooked Lane and then at Bridge Street. He decided to concentrate on the latter business and, in 1849, handed over the Bull Street business to his nephew, Richard Cadbury Barrow. In 1880, T. Plevins, on behalf of Richard Barrow, made a building application to build new premises in the newly formed Corporation Street, linked to the Bull Street shop. This new building was named Lancaster Buildings, but was known as Barrows, which became a store with a very high reputation and of which I have fond memories, as I lunched there often in the 1950s and early 1960s in the dining room reserved for men. After the building was demolished in the 1960s, Barrows moved into a new building on the other side of Bull Street, but it was not the same and no other store has replaced it.

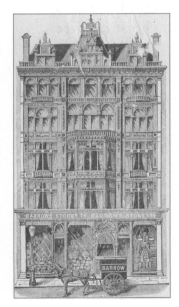

74–8 Corporation Street.

52–72 Corporation Street.

52–72 Corporation Street. This was a large development, known as County Chambers, stretching down Martineau Street as well, and incorporating sixteen shops and offices. The architect was J.P. Sharp & Co. who moved into the building from 46 Cherry Street when it was completed.

The building of 1888 was owned by Corporation Street Estate Co. It was five storeys high along Corporation Street but reduced in height as it went down Martineau Street. It was a worthy but unexciting building.

Other demolished buildings of Corporation Street mentioned in this book are: 53–7, Cobden Temperance Hotel and 118–?, Stork Hotel, which are covered in the chapter on Hotels and 132–48, Grand Theatre, which is covered in the chapter Places of Entertainment.

NEW STREET

The numbering starts from High Street and from there goes up the right side before returning down the other side towards Worcester Street.

8–19 New Street. These three buildings were all designed by Newton & Cheatle and were covered by five building applications, made between 1898 and 1901. The buildings included the City and Midland Arcades and, as can be seen from the photograph, were a great asset to the street scene. Unfortunately, they were destroyed in an air raid in April 1941 and all that remains is a short length of City Arcade opening off Union Street.

8–19 New Street, 1904.

Interior of City Arcade.

20–4 New Street.

20–4 New Street. Samuel Hyam moved his business from 116 New Street to 23 New Street, on the corner of Union Passage, some time between 1835 and 1839. During the late 1850s or early 1860s, Hyam commissioned J.J. Bateman to design a new building covering nos 20–4 New Street, with Hyam & Co. occupying nos 21–3. An opening was provided between nos 23 and 24 at ground floor level, giving access to Union Passage.

The building, as seen in the photograph above, was in a French Renaissance style and rather overshadowed its more delicate neighbour to the left. Hyam & Co. traded here until the late 1920s when the shop was taken over by Horne Brothers, who stayed there until the premises were demolished in the 1950s when they moved into the replacement building, in roughly the same position, but now numbered 14–15. S.N. Cooke, who had the shop at no. 20, was there from the beginning, right through until the rebuilding began.

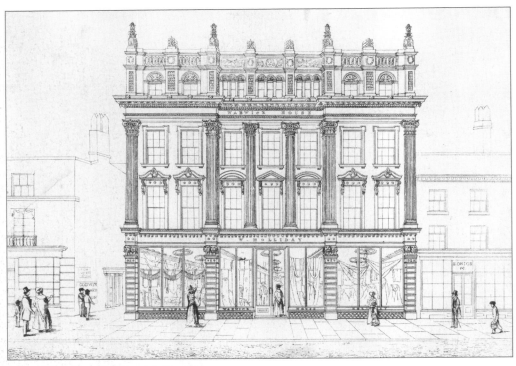

25–30 New Street – Warwick House.

25–30 New Street. The illustration shows the drawing of the first phase of the Classical-style development carried out by William Holliday in New Street. This section was designed by W. Thomas in 1839 and covered nos 28–30. By 1852 the firm had become Holliday & Lewis and during this period the building was doubled in size, the second phase matching the first. The partnership later became Holliday, Son & Co. and the building was known as Warwick House. At the beginning of the 1880s the building extended into the new thoroughfare known as Corporation Street. At about the same time as Hyam & Co. gave way to Horne Brothers, Holliday, Son & Co. was succeeded by Marshall & Snelgrove, who later took over no. 24. The premises were replaced in the 1940s.

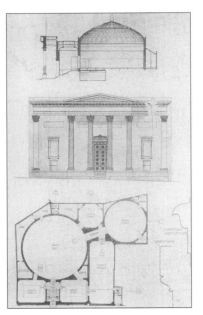

Royal Birmingham Society of Artists. The Royal Birmingham Society of Artists was formed from the Birmingham Academy of Arts, which had its first exhibition of pictures in a room in Union Passage on 12 September 1814.

Plans for the Royal Birmingham Society of Artists.

The Royal Birmingham Society of Artists.

The beautiful Classical-style building, with the portico extending over the pavement, was designed for the society by Rickman & Hussey and opened in 1829. The plan shows the interesting sequence of rooms, including the circular exhibition room, 52ft in diameter, with a dome roof.

Unfortunately, the building was demolished in 1912 and the society moved into galleries in a replacement block, devoted mainly to shops and offices.

73–9 New Street. Christ Church Buildings extended along New Street and curved round into and along Victoria Square. It was built in 1900 to replace Christ Church, mentioned later in the book, and was best known as Galloway's Corner, named after the photographic shop located on the bend.

The building was designed by Essex, Nicol & Goodman, in the practice's usual busy style. Among the shops was a Lyons' Corner House, a popular meeting place, particularly as there were several bus stops in the vicinity. The premises were demolished in 1970 and the site is now landscaped.

Christ Church Buildings.

We cross to the other side of the street, not having to bother about the traffic which abounded when these buildings were still standing.

The **New Royal Hotel** was an eighteenth-century building, which doubtless had a blameless life as a hotel, although I am in no position to confirm or deny it.

In about 1830 it made a career change and was occupied by the Post Office until 1874 when the organisation moved into a purpose-built building opposite the Town Hall. The building was then demolished and replaced.

The New Royal Hotel.

Exchange Buildings.

Exchange Buildings. It may seem wrong to include a building which had its principal entrance in Stephenson Place in this section, but it did have a substantial presence in New Street and an entrance to part of the building. The foundation stone of the building was laid on 21 January 1863 and it was opened by the Mayor, H. Wiggin Esq., on 2 January 1865. The architect was Edward Holmes who also designed the Classical-style bank (now a bookshop), on the opposite corner of New Street and Stephenson Place. The cost of the building was £19,300. The building was extended along New Street in 1877–8, the architect being J.A. Chatwin. The ground floor was fronted by shops with the Exchange Room and Chamber of Commerce behind. On the floor above was a large assembly room, entered from New Street. The upper floors housed refreshment, coffee and smoking rooms and suites of offices. The building, having just achieved its centenary, was demolished in 1965.

Attwood & Spooner's Bank opened at 131 New Street in 1791 and carried on sedately, as far as the public was concerned, until 10 March 1865, when it suspended payments and was found to have liabilities of almost £1,000,000. The business was taken over by the Joint Stock Banking Company, which paid a dividend of 11*s* 3*d* in the pound for the assets and property.

Attwood & Spooner's Bank
at 131 New Street.

The original bank premises were replaced by a new building, designed by F.B. Osborn, and erected in 1875. The bank was later taken over by Lloyds Bank and a new larger building replaced it in 1919, designed by P.B. Chatwin. This later building was demolished in 1970 and the bank moved into the Rotunda.

Other demolished New Street buildings mentioned in this book include: Christ Church covered in the chapter Religious Buildings; Colonnade and Hen & Chickens Hotels covered in the Hotels chapter; Theatre Royal covered in the chapter Places of Entertainment and the King Edward VI School is covered in Educational Buildings.

Birmingham Joint Stock Bank.

OTHER CITY CENTRE BUILDINGS

29–37 Temple Row. This distinguished terrace of five houses was built in 1715, or soon after, and was designed by William Westley, also responsible for the Old Square. Dr John Ash, the founder of the General Hospital, lived at no. 37 at one time, prior to moving to Ashted. In later years the houses were used for offices and remained until giving way graciously (no other way for such an elegant building) to allow Rackham's to be built

29–37 Temple Row.

64 and 65 High Street. John Taylor and Sampson Lloyd III opened the first proper bank in Birmingham at this address on 3 June 1765, under the title of Taylor & Lloyd. It continued under that name until the Taylor family withdrew its interest a century after its opening. The bank still operates having changed its title to Lloyds TSB. The building was the head office of the bank from 1815 until 1871 when a new head office was erected in Colmore Row (to be mentioned shortly). The branch closed on 17 October 1942.

The Old Bank, 64 and 65 High Street, 1939.

Birmingham Canal Navigation Office, Paradise Row, 1907.

Birmingham Canal Navigation Office, Paradise Row. A bill for making a navigable canal from Birmingham to Wolverhampton was introduced in Parliament in 1868 and received the Royal Assent on 26 July. The engineer for the project was James Brindley and the first boat-load of coal (the main reason for building the canal), was delivered on 7 November 1769. An office was built at the western end of Paradise Row (now Paradise Street) and wharves were constructed on the south side of Broad Street. This fascinating building closed in 1912 and was demolished.

The Old Library, 24 Union Street. The Birmingham Library was founded in 1779 and its first meeting place was in Snow Hill, where it was open for one hour each morning. A move was made to larger premises in Upper Priory on 5 May 1790 and, by then, the opening hours were much longer. Land was obtained on a 120-year lease, commencing 24 June 1793, from Dr Withering, at a ground rent of £11 15s per annum. Building work started quickly, but the library, designed by William Hollins and built in stone, was not completed until 1797. The building was

The Old Library, 24 Union Street.

symmetrical about the portico and was extended later to the left. A new building was erected in Margaret Street in 1899 where the library remains as part of the Birmingham and Midland Institute. No. 24 Union Street remained in use until it was demolished in the 1960s.

The first part of **New Street station** was opened on 1 June 1854 having been built by the London & North Western Railway. The main feature of the station was its roof of iron and glass which had a single span of 212ft and was 1,080ft long. The station was extended in 1880 on the other side of Great Queen Street, which was converted to Queen's Drive, and the central access bridge to the tracks stretched from the Stephenson Place booking hall to Station Street and was also a public right of way. The station was damaged during the war and was replaced by a new building in the 1960s. The aerial photograph shows the three sections of the station. On the left is the Queen's Hotel, next to which is the long, rectangular-shaped roof covering the first phase of the station erected in 1854. On the right the curved roofs cover the 1880 extension.

New Street station, 1900.

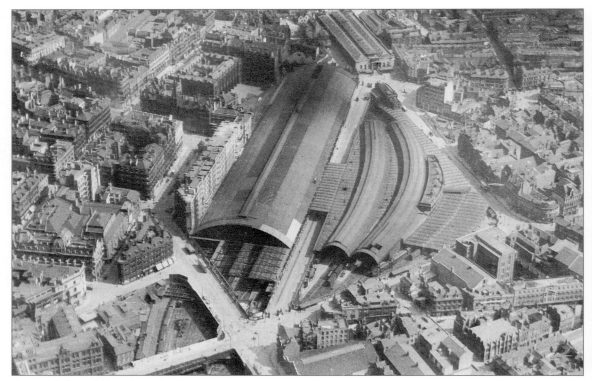

An aerial shot of New Street station.

Birmingham & Midland Institute, Ratcliffe Place/Paradise Street.

Birmingham & Midland Institute, Ratcliffe Place/Paradise Street. At a meeting of the Philosophical Institution in Cannon Street on 10 January 1853, a decision was taken to found what later became the Birmingham & Midland Institute. Fund raising was started immediately, and included three readings by Charles Dickens, at Christmas, at the Town Hall and £227 19s 9d was raised. A vacant plot of land by the Town Hall, between Paradise Street and Edmund Street, had been selected and Royal Assent was given to the bill proposing this on 3 July 1854. The proposed building was designed by E.M. Barry and the foundation stone of the first phase, starting at Paradise Street, was laid by the Prince Consort on 22 November 1855 and the building was opened in 1856.

Among the institute's early Presidents were Charles Dickens and Charles Kingsley. The remaining land along Ratcliffe Place had been used for the Birmingham Central Library and so, when the institute decided to extend in 1881, it was carried out along Paradise Street. The building was designed by Martin & Chamberlain in a Gothic style that disowned its parent. The buildings were demolished in 1965 and the institute took over the building of the Birmingham Library in Margaret Street and is still there.

28 Union Street. This building erected in the late 1850s was one of the first designed by John Henry Chamberlain in Birmingham and was for shop premises for his uncle. At the time of erection the name of the firm was Eld & Chamberlain. By 1864 it was Chamberlain & King and by 1883 it had become Chamberlain, King & Jones.

28 Union Street.

Snow Hill station. The building of a second rail route between London and Birmingham was initiated in 1846 by the Birmingham & Oxford Junction Railway, which was later absorbed by the Great Western Railway. Consequently, the track was built to the broad gauge width of 7ft ¼in. The station opened in October 1852 served by a wooden structure until permanent buildings were erected in 1871. In 1854 another line was added with mixed gauge tracks and from 1 November 1868 all trains to London ran on the standard gauge track. In 1905, the hotel (mentioned later) closed except for the dining room and the station was rebuilt between 1906 and 1912,

utilising the hotel building for administrative offices. Main line trains ceased to use Snow Hill in 1967 and the hotel and booking hall were demolished in 1969. The last train used the station on 4 March 1872 and demolition of the station began in 1977. However a new station has been built on the site and, with the revival in train travel, should have a bright future.

Snow Hill station.

Lloyds Bank, Colmore Row.

Lloyds Bank, on the corner of Eden Place, was designed by J.A. Chatwin and opened in 1871. It was the head office of the bank in Birmingham but, unfortunately, was demolished in the early 1960s and replaced by a less attractive building.

95 Colmore Row.

95 Colmore Row. This building, on the corner of Newhall Street, was designed by Frank B. Osborn in 1878. I worked in the building, in the corner office on the fourth floor, between 1954 and 1958. From there I could look down at the Union Club on the opposite corner of Newhall Street, where Frank Osborn had died at luncheon on 6 April 1907. The building was replaced by the National Westminster building, designed by John Madin, in the early 1970s.

The **Liberal Club** building, known later as Norwich Union Chambers, was designed by Jethro Cossins and built in 1885 at a cost of £60,000. The building became available soon after completion owing to the split in the Liberal Party over Home Rule for Ireland, and was taken on lease by King Edward VI School for Girls who decided it could be adapted to accommodate 300 pupils. The alterations were carried out under the direction of J.A. Chatwin and the building was ready for the school by autumn 1888. After a few years, the school bought land at the rear of the Hen & Chickens Hotel, adjoining the Boys' School, in New Street and a new building was erected there, to which the school moved on 6 November 1896. The building was bought later by Norwich Union and was eventually demolished, with its neighbours, in 1965.

The Liberal Club, Congreve Street.

Staffordshire Bank, Colmore Row. William Doubleday was the architect of this Classical-style building built for the Staffordshire Bank in 1887 and it was a complete change from his design for the nearby Cobden Hotel, mentioned later in the chapter Hotels and Public Houses. The building was taken over by the Bank of England, as its third site in Birmingham, in 1890 and was demolished early in 1973 after the bank moved to new premises on the corner of Temple Row and Cherry Street.

Staffordshire Bank, Colmore Row.

Buckler & Webb, 47 and 49 Church Street. Newton & Cheatle designed many fine buildings on the Colmore Estate between 1897 and 1902 but this is the only one that I know that has been demolished. It was built in 1898 and was one of three in line, all different and all of quality. Its demolition in the early 1970s was sad and the replacement building, by James A. Roberts, was out of place.

Buckler & Webb, 47 and 49 Church Street.

Wesleyan & General Assurance Society, Steelhouse Lane. Ewen Harper submitted a building application for premises in Steelhouse Lane, on behalf of the Wesleyan & General Assurance Society in December 1901 and the society moved into the new building, from its offices at 131–51 Corporation Street.

Many other city centre buildings have been covered in subsequent chapters, but I have not listed them here as there are too many.

Wesleyan & General Assurance Society, Steelhouse Lane.

TWO

Public Buildings

GENERAL

The Market Cross, Old Cross or Butter Cross (for it answered to all these names), was situated in the middle of the Bull Ring, roughly where, later, Nelson's statue stood, when first erected. The building was an arcaded shelter for market workers, to which an upper room was added in 1703, at a cost of £80 9s 1d. This room was used for the Court Leet and for the conduct of public business and meetings. At a meeting on 21 July 1784, presumably in this building, it was decided that, owing to its ruinous state, it should be demolished. This was carried out the next month.

Market Cross, Bull Ring.

THE WELSH CROSS.

The Welsh Cross, Dale End.

The Welsh Cross (or I have seen Welch Cross), situated close to the junction with High Street and Bull Street, was similar to the Market Cross, but smaller, with an arcaded shelter at ground level, to which an upper room was added in 1706 to serve as a military guardhouse. The building was demolished in March 1803.

The workhouse was built at the lower end of Lichfield Street, near to Steelhouse Lane in 1733, at a cost of £1,173 3s 5d. Two wings were added; one on the left in 1766 at a cost of £400 for use as an infirmary, and the other on the right, added in 1779 at a cost of £700 as a place of labour. At this time it accommodated 600 and the intention was to employ every able-bodied pauper and drive away the idle and profligate. A new workhouse was built on Birmingham Heath in 1851 and the original building was demolished in 1853.

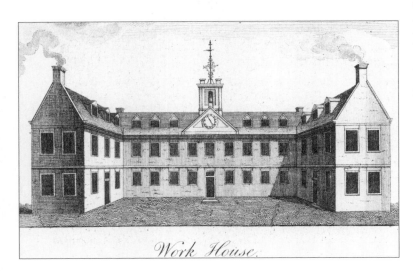

Work House.

The Workhouse, Lichfield Street.

The Old Prison, Pleck Lane. At a public meeting on 9 September 1733, held in the upper room of the Old Cross, it was decided to build a prison in Pleck Lane and the building was extended in 1757. Conditions in the prison were revolting and were condemned by the prison reformer John Howard, following inspections he made in 1779 and 1788. The building was demolished in 1806 following the building of a new prison in Moor Street, and the building materials were sold for £250.

The Old Prison, Pleck Lane.

Cavalry Barracks, Great Brook Street, Ashted. Following riots in Birmingham in 1791, it was decided that barracks were needed nearby and a site was offered in Ashted covering 4 acres of land. The site was bounded by roads on all sides; Great Brook Street to the north, Windsor Street to the west, Barrack Street to the east and Vauxhall Road to the south. The main building, facing Great Brook Street, was three storeys high and there were two-storey blocks down the east and west sides. The first stone was laid on 28 August 1792 and the building work was completed in the summer of 1793. The building cost was £13,000 and the barracks accommodated 162 men. The barracks disappeared in the early 1930s.

Cavalry Barracks, Great Brook Street, Ashted.

Public Office and Prison, Moor Street, 1890.

The Public Office and Prison was designed by William Hollins and cost nearly £11,000 to build; there was some comment that it was too ornate for the purpose it had to serve.

There was a rusticated ground floor, having two wide openings with segmental heads, and a lofty, upper floor, divided into six bays separated by paired Ionic half columns. The ground floor contained offices, with a magistrates' court on the first floor and the prison was located at the rear of the site.

The prison opened on 29 September 1806 but it was over a year later, on 19 October 1807, before the public office opened for business. A police station, designed by D.R. Hill, was added in 1847.

The building became inadequate to carry out its functions satisfactorily and it was with some relief that the Council House and Victoria Law Courts were built to take up the burden. The last mention of use as public offices is 1894, but the police station, at the rear of the site, was in use into the early years of the twentieth century.

The Central Fire Station was designed by Martin & Chamberlain and erected in 1883. Two problems had emerged by the 1930s relating to the site: it was not large enough and it was in the wrong place, as traffic congestion made the fire brigade's rapid response to emergencies difficult to achieve on too many occasions. A new building was erected on land between Corporation Street and Aston Street, which opened in 1935 and is still in use today.

Central Fire Station, Upper Priory.

Police Court, Station Street, Sutton Coldfield. This building, erected at the end of the 1880s, acted both as court and police station, with the court on the first floor and the police station on the ground floor. It closed in 1960 and was demolished in 1967.

Police Court, Station Street, Sutton Coldfield. *(Supplied by Sutton Coldfield Reference Library)*

LIBRARIES

Adderley Park, Saltley. This building was erected by Lord Norton in Adderley Park as a public library and museum, and was taken over by the Council and opened as a free library on 11 January 1864. I have seen G.E. Street named as the architect, but would have thought more would have been made of it if that was the case. The building was demolished in the mid-1990s.

Adderley Park,
Saltley, 1913.

The Central Library was erected on land owned by the Birmingham & Midland Institute with the condition that it was built to match the appearance of the adjoining institute building. E.M. Barry, who had designed the institute's building, was appointed as architect. However, his proposals were too expensive and he was replaced by William Martin. The building had two parts: the Central and Western Lending Library which opened on 6 September 1865 and the Reference Library, which opened on 26 October 1866. On 11 January 1879, a fire started in the reference library, destroying the building and most of the collection, although most of the books in the lending library were saved. The building was rebuilt, designed by Martin & Chamberlain, and was opened on 1 June 1882. It was replaced by the present library in 1973.

The interior of the
Reference Library.

Legge Street/Aston Road, Gosta Green, 1910.

The foundation stone of the **Gosta Green, or Eastern, library** was laid on 26 October 1866, the day that the Reference and Southern Libraries were opened. The building was designed by Bateman & Corser and was opened to the public in June 1868.

The first public library, the **Northern**, was opened in **Constitution Hill** in April 1861, in an existing building. When the lease expired in 1881 it was replaced by a new building, also in Constitution Hill, designed by Martin & Chamberlain. The building was demolished in the middle of the 1960s.

Northern Library,
Constitution Hill, 1910.

PUBLIC BATHS

Kent Street Baths. Following an Enabling Act of Parliament in 1846, the council instructed Daniel R. Hill to design public baths on a site in Kent Street. The foundation stone of the building (the estimated cost of which was £10,000), was laid on 29 October 1849 by the Mayor, Mr S. Thornton, and the baths were opened to the public on 12 May 1851. The building provided two swimming baths, sixty-nine private baths and three plunge baths. There was also a washing department with twenty-five washing stalls and thirty-two drying horses. However, the stalls were little used and the area was converted into Turkish baths in 1878. A Gala Bath was built in 1933, next door to the existing building, built in stone in a Classical style, contrasting with the brick, Gothic style of the original. The baths were demolished in the mid-1970s.

Kent Street Baths.

Monument Road, Ladywood. These baths were the last built by Birmingham in the Victorian era and were designed by Martin & Chamberlain. The building was opened on 27 February 1883 and contained first- and second-class swimming pools and washing and bathing facilities. This building was replaced by a new building, which opened on 27 June 1940, and provided only one swimming pool, owing to intended road-widening proposals. The new building tried hard but just failed to last as long as its predecessor, being demolished in 1994.

Monument Road, Ladywood.

Victoria Road, Aston. These baths, built in red brick and terra cotta, were opened on 5 October 1892. It is best remembered, as far as I am concerned at least, as the place I went to for swimming lessons, from school, before the Second World War, but even this didn't save the building from demolition, which took place in about 1970.

Victoria Road, Aston.

MARKETS

Market Hall, High Street. The Market Hall, on the corner of Bell Street and stretching through to Worcester Street, was very much a part of the Bull Ring, despite its address, and was one of Birmingham's best known and best loved buildings. It was built in stone in the Classical style and the architect was Charles Edge.

The building was 365ft long and 108ft wide and the cost of the building was £67,261. The foundation stone was laid in February 1833 and the building was opened to the public on 12 February 1835. Improvements were made in 1851 and a bronze fountain was erected in the centre of the hall to commemorate this final act by the Street Commissioners and this was inaugurated on 24 December 1851.

The Market Hall was badly damaged in an air raid in August 1940, but continued to operate as an open-air market until the early 1960s when it was demolished to make way for the Inner Ring Road.

Market Hall, High Street, 1901.

St Martin's Meat Market, Jamaica Row. One of the last acts of the Street Commissioners was to build this meat market on the corner of Dean Street and opposite Smithfield Market. It was opened in 1851 and operated until November 1897, when it closed after the building of its successor in Bradford Street.

St Martin's Meat Market, Jamaica Row.

The Wholesale Fish Market was built on the corner of the Bull Ring on the opposite side of Bell Street from the Market Hall. The architect was J.J. Bateman and the foundation stone was laid on 14 July 1870. A large extension was added in 1884, designed by W. Spooner Till, the Borough Surveyor. The building disappeared, together with the other buildings in the Bull Ring and with Bell Street itself, to make way for the 1960s redevelopment.

Fish Market, Bell Street, 1900.

Wholesale Vegetable Market, Moat Lane, 1973.

Wholesale Vegetable Market, Moat Lane. Smithfield Market, as it came to be called, was opened in 1817, after the Street Commissioners acquired the site of the old Birmingham Manor House early in the nineteenth century and filled in the moat. The site was used for the sale of cattle, horses, pigs and sheep, together with hay and straw. In 1883–4, W. Spooner Till designed the Wholesale Vegetable Market on part of the site and, at the same time, F.B. Osborn & Reading added St Martin's Hotel and shops. The site was cleared for redevelopment soon after the photograph was taken.

Meat Market, Bradford Street. The Meat Market, built to replace the building in Jamaica Row, was built on a site occupied previously by the Circus Chapel and bounded at the rear by Cheapside and on the one side by Sherlock Street. It was designed by Essex, Nicol & Goodman in 1894–5 and opened in 1897.

Meat Market, Bradford Street.

THREE

Hospitals

General Hospital, Summer Lane. The first hospital built in Birmingham, with the exception of the Workshop Infirmary, was the General Hospital in Summer Lane (on the corner of Lower Loveday Street and with the Birmingham & Fazeley canal at the rear), on the initiative of Dr John Ash, a local physician. The first meeting to discuss the project was held on 21 November 1765 where substantial donations and annual subscriptions were promised and it was decided to proceed with the scheme. A site in Summer Lane, of about 8 acres, was selected and a plan for the building was prepared by a Mr Vyse. This was for a three-storey building, designed to accommodate 100 patients, and expected to cost about £3,000. Work started in 1766 but, by November, funds were almost exhausted and it was decided to stop for the winter. New funds were not forthcoming and it was 1777 before building work recommenced and the hospital opened formally on 20 August 1779, although with only forty beds available. In 1790 two side wings, two storeys high, were added. Later extensions included a new wing containing twenty bed spaces, dispensary, physicians' and surgeons' room and other offices added by William Martin in 1857 and nurses' homes and burns wards added by Yeoville Thomason in 1880. The hospital closed after the new General Hospital in Steelhouse Lane opened in 1897 and the site was subsequently occupied by a power station.

General Hospital,
Summer Lane.

Birmingham General Dispensary, 4 Union Street.

Birmingham General Dispensary, 4 Union Street. A proposal to start a dispensary in Birmingham was first raised in 1792 and received support, notably from Matthew Boulton. A house was taken in Temple Row in 1794 with the aim of providing medical relief as needed for the poorer classes. The number of cases increased steadily and the house became inadequate for its purpose and a site was found in Union Street on which a new building was erected. The building, designed by William Hollins in a Classical style and not admired by R.K. Dent, opened in 1806. Dent may not have admired the building but he did admire the services provided inside and this was exemplified by the following figures. The number of patients seen in 1794 was 280 and in 1877 19,286 patients were treated. By that time the total number of patients treated was: sick: 345,881; midwifery: 35,123; inoculation: 101,387. The dispensary continued in Union Street until the mid-1920s and then moved to Steelhouse Lane, on the corner of Upper Priory, in the building erected as the Out-Patients' Department of the Birmingham Children's Hospital. The dispensary left there during the Second World War.

Eye Infirmary, Cannon Street. The first Eye Infirmary in Birmingham opened in Cannon Street in 1824 before moving to the building belonging to the Polytechnic Institution in Steelhouse Lane after the institution closed in September 1853. The institution building was purchased for the Children's Hospital in 1861 and the Eye Infirmary moved into the front portion of the Royal Hotel in Temple Row before moving to a new building in Church Street, designed by Payne & Talbot, and opened in 1883.

Eye Infirmary, Cannon Street.

Appropriately, this building is now occupied by the Hotel Du Vin and the Eye Hospital is situated at the City Hospital, Dudley Road.

The Orthopaedic and Spinal Hospital had many homes until moving in to Great Charles Street in 1858 into premises previously occupied by the Institution of Mechanical Engineers, situated on the corner of Newhall Street. The premises also housed the Ear and Throat Infirmary until its move to its new building in Edmund Street, on the corner of Barwick Street, in 1891.

The Royal Orthopaedic Hospital, which it became, had subsequent moves to Broad Street and to The Woodlands, Bristol Road, Northfield, where it is still based.

Orthopaedic Hospital, Great Charles Street.

Out-Patients' Department, Children's Hospital, Steelhouse Lane. This building, on the corner of Upper Priory, was designed by Martin & Chamberlain in 1869, with extensions added in 1875. The In-Patients' Department was situated on the opposite side of Steelhouse Lane in the old Polytechnic Institution building, previously occupied by the Eye Infirmary, where it had been since 1861. However, within a year it had moved to the premises in Broad Street, previously used as a Lying in Hospital to provide maternity care for sick women. The Out-Patients' Department stayed at the Steelhouse Lane address until the mid-1920s and then moved to the comparatively new Children's Hospital, designed by Martin & Martin, on Ladywood Road. The old building was taken over by the Birmingham General Dispensary until the early 1940s.

Out-Patients' Department, Children's Hospital, Steelhouse Lane.

Homeopathic Hospital, Easy Row.

Homeopathic Hospital, Easy Row. Homeopathy was started in a dispensary in Great Charles Street in 1845, but moved to more convenient premises, in a house in Old Square in May 1847. Later, a site was acquired in Easy Row and the first stage of a new building, designed by Yeoville Thomason, was erected and opened on 23 November 1873.

Extensions, designed by Crouch & Butler, were added in 1898 and 1901. The building closed as a hospital in the late 1940s but was used for other purposes for another ten years, before being demolished.

Mental Asylum, Rubery Hill. The existing Lunatic Asylum, in Lodge Road, was not able to cope with the number of inmates and so an additional asylum was built at Rubery Hill in 1882 at a cost of £132,000, which seems an enormous cost to me. The premises were designed by Martin & Chamberlain, who were also responsible for extensions in 1890 and 1893. The hospital closed down in the early 1990s and all that remains are the Chapel, the Lodge at Bristol Road South and the Medical Superintendent's House, all listed grade II.

Mental Asylum, Rubery Hill.

Jaffray Hospital, built in red brick and terra cotta and designed by Yeoville Thomason, was erected in 1884–5 and the building and furnishings were paid for by John Jaffray. The hospital, standing in 8 acres of grounds, was opened officially on 29 November 1885 by the Prince of Wales. It closed in 1991 and was demolished about four years later.

Jaffray Hospital, Jaffray Road, Erdington.

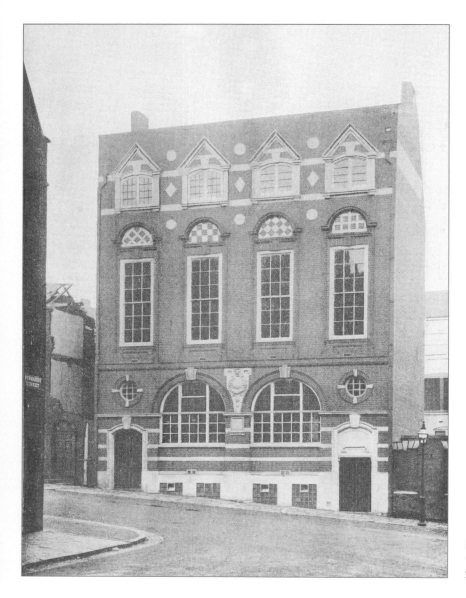

Dental Hospital,
132 Great Charles
Street.

The first **Dental Hospital** opened at 13 Temple Street in 1857, complete with two chairs and no anaesthetic. From there it moved to Broad Street in 1871 and a chloroformist was appointed. I have not managed to find its address in Broad Street but by 1890 the hospital was at 71 Newhall Street, where it stayed until it moved into a purpose-built hospital at 132 Great Charles Street, opened by Sir Oliver Lodge, in July 1905. The architectural practice of Bateman & Bateman was the winner of a limited competition to design the building which cost about £10,000 to erect. The facing materials were thin, red Ruabon bricks, with Portland stone dressings. The building disappeared with the radical changes to that end and side of Great Charles Street in the early 1960s and the hospital moved to its present premises at St Chad's Queensway.

FOUR

Educational Buildings

BOARD SCHOOLS

The Elementary Education Act of 1870 empowered each local authority to elect a School Board with the responsibility of providing a school place for each child in the district where these places did not previously exist. The schools that were built were called Board Schools and this system continued until the Education Act of 1902 abolished School Boards and placed the responsibility for education directly with local authorities.

Within the present boundary of Birmingham, six School Boards were formed, namely: Birmingham, Harborne, Aston, Kings Norton, Yardley and Handsworth. The Harborne School Board looked after Harborne and Smethwick, and after Harborne was taken into Birmingham in 1891 the name of the board was changed to Smethwick, which was more appropriate as that was where most of its work had always been concentrated.

During the time of the existence of School Boards, eighty-seven new schools were built in present-day Birmingham and in addition, several existing buildings were modified and used. Over half of these schools were built by the Birmingham School Board and these came to be recognised as 'The Best Building in the Neighbourhood'.

Despite this, I have had some difficulty in finding photographs, resulting in an unequal balance between School Boards. Most of the photographs have been taken at the time the schools were due to be demolished.

Farm Street School, opened in 1873 for 1,055 pupils.

Osler Street School, opened in 1875 for 1,025 pupils. It was known later as Follett Osler School.

Cowper Street School, opened in 1885 for 1,010 pupils.

Smith Street School, opened in 1876 for 972 pupils.

Camden Street School, opened in 1890 for 1,090 pupils.

The five schools pictured on pp. 43–4 were built for the Birmingham School Board and all were designed by Martin & Chamberlain. The practice designed all but four of the board's schools, from 1900 under the name of Martin & Martin. All of the schools had extensions, those carried out before 1902 being designed by the practice.

The next five schools were all for Aston School Board.

Alma Street. Opened in 1878 for 1,023 pupils and designed by William Jenkins.

Vicarage Road. Opened in 1878 for 720 pupils and designed by Edward Holmes. There were extensions in 1880, for 510 infants, and again in 1881 and 1894. It was known later as Manor Park School.

Left: Upper Thomas Street. Opened in 1878 for 1,003 pupils and designed by William Jenkins. It was extended in 1885–6 to add 300 pupils and was altered in 1898.

Lozells Street. Opened in 1882 for 1,015 pupils and designed by William Jenkins. The school was extended in 1886 including the provision of a kitchen to allow for cookery classes.

Aston Lane. Opened in 1886 for 1,008 pupils and designed by Edward Holmes. It was extended in 1890 and its name was changed in 1935 to Aston Hall Junior and Infant School.

High Street, Kings Heath.

High Street, Kings Heath. This school was built by the King's Heath School Board in 1878 for 493 pupils and was designed by William Hale. The site was enlarged in 1890 and extensions were added in 1890 and 1895, both by Edward Holmes.

Birchfield Road. This school, built by the Handsworth School Board, opened in 1895. The architect was John P. Osborne and accommodated 660 pupils in the first phase and it was extended the following year to complete the original design.

Birchfield Road.

OTHER SCHOOLS AND COLLEGES

Free Grammar School, New Street. The property of the Gild of the Holy Cross, which had been seized by King Henry VIII, was returned to the town by King Edward VI for the purpose of establishing a grammar school and this was started in the hall of the Gild, a timber structure. This building served until 1707 when it was replaced, on the same site, by a two-storey building with side wings projecting to the pavement and a central entrance tower containing a figure of Edward VI, a clock and a bell. This building was demolished in 1832 and the boys were taught in the Shakespeare Rooms, New Street, until the new school was built. A competition was held, attracting more than sixty entrants, to select a design for the new school. The scheme submitted by Charles Barry was chosen. The impressive, Gothic-style, two-storey high building, was quadrangular in plan being 174ft long to the street and 125ft deep. Not only was there a new building but also, a new curriculum, as Latin and Greek were joined by other subjects that may not have been of such high class but may have proved more useful. At what time the name of the school was recognised generally by the name of its founder I do not know. Charles Barry

Free Grammar School, New Street.

The original school building.

received assistance in carrying out the building from Augustus Welby Pugin, a collaboration that was to be repeated soon afterwards in the building of the Houses of Parliament. The building graced New Street until 1936 when it was demolished and the school moved to new premises at Edgbaston where it remains today.

The Blue Coat Charity School opened on 9 August 1724, the architect of the building being John Rawsthorne. The school was intended for orphans and children of the poor and provided clothing, maintenance, a good elementary education and religious instruction according to the principles of the Church of England. The figures of a boy and girl above the entrance were added in 1770 and were sculpted by Edward Grubb. Extensions and improvements were carried out in 1794 at a cost of £2,800.

Blue Coat School, St Philip's Churchyard.

The Blue Coat Charity School.

At fourteen, the children went to work, often, particularly in the case of girls, into domestic service. The children wore a distinctive blue uniform into the twentieth century, based on the eighteenth-century original. The school, including the statues, moved to new buildings, designed by J.L. Ball and H.W. Simister, at Somerset Road, Harborne in 1930.

Protestant Dissenting Charity School, Graham Street. The foundation of this school was started in 1760 by Unitarians, when they established a Free School for boys and girls, with part of the time devoted to work employment to prepare them for the future.

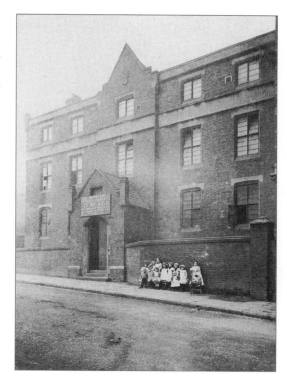

Protestant Dissenting Charity School, Graham Street.

A building was bought in Park Street in 1791 and the number of pupils was increased to thirty-six boys and eighteen girls. This was followed in 1839 by the erection of a new building in Graham Street, designed by D.R. Hill, and all of the pupils were girls. The school closed just before, or soon after, the start of the First World War.

The Birmingham & Edgbaston Proprietary School was established in 1838 for the sons of wealthy non-conformists. The school building was designed by Hugh Smith in an Elizabethan style, faced with red bricks and stone dressings, and opened in 1841.

The building is better remembered as the home of King Edward's Grammar School, Five Ways, a role it performed from 1883 until 1958 when the school moved to Scotland Lane, Bartley Green.

Birmingham & Edgbaston Proprietary School, Hagley Road, Five Ways.

The foundation stone of the **Free Industrial School**, designed by C.W. Orford, was laid on 12 April 1849. It had started in 1846 in a workshop in Lichfield Street, as St Philip's Ragged School. For some years it gave education to children of soldiers killed in the Crimean War and, after that ceased, an application was made for a certificate under the Industrial Schools Act of 1866. This was granted in March 1868. In later years the site housed council schools for deaf and dumb children and for mentally deficient children.

Free Industrial School, Gem Street.

Mason College, Edmund Street. The foundation stone of the Science College was laid on 23 February 1875, but this impressive building, designed by Jethro Cossins, was not completed and opened until 1880. The college was founded and endowed by Josiah Mason, became a University College in 1896 and the first home of Birmingham University in 1900.

The site was too cramped for the long-term future of the university and a move was made to Edgbaston where the first buildings were opened officially by King Edward VII on 7 July 1909. Mason College was still used until 1961, not long before it was demolished.

Mason College, Edmund Street.

Bourne College, Quinton.

Bourne College was established in 1876 for sons of Primitive Methodists and was named after Hugh Bourne (1772–1852), a founder of Primitive Methodism. The redundant St Chad's Grammar School was used at first, but 19 acres of land at Quinton was bought and E. Walton was appointed to design the new building, the foundation stone of which was laid on 6 June 1881. The college closed in 1928 and, after rebuilding, opened in 1931 as Quinton Hall, a residential home for elderly men. The home closed and the premises were sold in 1981 and the site was developed for residential use.

The Central Technical College, designed by Essex, Nicol & Goodman, was opened on 13 December 1895, having cost £90,000 to build and equip. It also housed Central Secondary School for Boys and City of Birmingham Commercial College before the building was demolished to make way for the Inner Ring Road.

Central Technical College, Suffolk Street.

FIVE

Religious Buildings

CHURCH OF ENGLAND

St Bartholomew's Church was built in 1749, on land donated by the Jennens family, as a chapel of ease to St Martin and became a parish church in 1847. It was built in a Classical style and was a plain rectangle in plan. The gabled ends had plain parapets with ornamental urns at each end. There were three doors, with pedimented heads at the nominal west end (as the church was built to line up with the street rather than align the church to position the altar at the east end), and with a small clock tower, cupola and weather vane above the larger, central door. Along each side were two levels of nine, round-headed windows, the upper ones being taller than those at the lower level. The church was restored in 1893, closed in 1937 and was demolished by 1943.

St Bartholomew, Masshouse Lane.

St Mary's Church, Whittall Street was built in 1774 on land given by Dorothy and Mary Weaman, as a chapel of ease to St Martin, and became a parish church in 1841. It was an octagonal brick building in the Classical style comprising chancel, nave, side aisle and gallery. It had seating for nearly 1,700 people and was designed by Joseph Pickford.

On 6 January 1776 part of the gallery collapsed during Divine Service, but no one suffered serious injury. At the west end there was a three-stage tower: round, then octagonal with Doric columns at each angle, then octagonal again with clock face and pediment to alternate faces, surmounted with a spire. The tower was rebuilt

St Mary's Church.

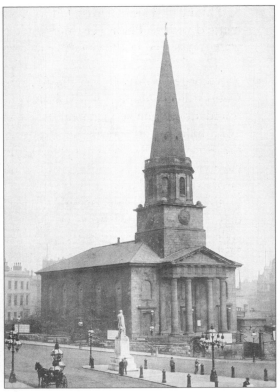

Christ Church, Colmore Row.

in 1866 with small changes. The interior was described as spacious but somewhat gloomy from the smallness of the windows. The building was closed under an Act of 1925 to allow, I believe, for the extension of the General Hospital.

The building of **Christ Church**, designed by Charles Norton, began in 1805, the foundation stone being laid on 22 July followed by dinner at the Royal Hotel. A week later, the king gave a donation of £1,000 towards the erection of a Free Church. The building was consecrated on 6 July 1813, followed naturally, by dinner in the afternoon at the Royal Hotel. It was known as the Free Church, as the whole of the ground floor was used for free sittings and only the gallery seats could be reserved. On the ground floor the men were seated on the one side and the women on the other, which led to the following rhyme:

> The churches in general we everywhere find,
> Are places where men to the women are joined;
> But at *Christ Church it seems*, they are more cruel hearted,
> For men and their wives are brought here to be parted.

The building was of stone and the cost of the church was £26,000, a sum which was raised with some difficulty. It became a parish, assigned out of St Martin and

St Philip, in 1865. Christ Church was demolished in 1898 and the parish was merged with St Philip. The 600 interred bodies, including that of John Baskerville, were transferred to the cemetery in Warstone Lane.

St George's Church was the first church in Birmingham to be built under the Church Building Act of 1818 and was known as a Commissioners' church. The foundation stone was laid on 19 March 1820 and it was consecrated on 30 July 1822 followed afterwards, so as not to be outdone by Christ Church, by dinner at the Royal Hotel. The church, designed by Thomas Rickman, contained chancel, nave, aisles, organ chamber, vestry and west tower and was built for £12,481, a saving of over £1,100 on the original estimate. The facing material was stone and the style was described as 'Late Middle Pointed'. It became a parish, assigned out of St Martin, in 1830 and was enlarged in 1884. The church merged with St Edward's Church, New John Street West and was demolished in 1960. The name was transferred to St Edward's Church and is now borne by that church's successor, St George, Bridge Street West.

St George, Great Hampton Row/Tower Street.

St Peter, Dale End. The foundation stone of this Commissioners' church was laid on 26 July 1825 and it was consecrated on 10 August 1827. I have seen no mention of a dinner after the consecration but a select few had been to breakfast at the Royal Hotel before the laying of the foundation stone.

The church was designed by Rickman & Hutchinson in the Greek Revival style with a Doric portico and octagonal turret and was built in stone. The original estimate was £13,087 but it was built for £12,204 9s 4d.

It was destroyed by fire in January 1831 but was rebuilt by 1837. A parish was assigned out of St Philip in 1847 and the church was closed for demolition in 1899.

The Foundation was begun the 11th day of May, 1825. The first stone was laid the 26th day of July, 1825, by the Rev. Charles Curtis; Rev. Laurence Gardner, D. D.; and James Taylor, Esq. the local Commissioners for building Churches in this district. The Church was consecrated the 10th day of August, 1827, by the Honble & Right Rev. Henry Ryder, D. D., Lord Bishop of the Diocese. The total cost of erecting the Church amounted to £13,087. 12s. 3d. being £882. 10s. 8d. less than the approved Estimate; which sum, together with £5,718. the cost of site, was defrayed by his Majesty's Commissioners for Building new Churches, out of the Parliamentary grant of £1,000,000. The Church contains 1903 Sittings, of which 1381 are appropriated to the accommodation of the Poor.— Rev. L. Gardner, D. D., Rector of the parish. Rev. A. J. Clarke, A. M., Minister. J. W. Whateley and John Cope, Esqs. Churchwardens. --- Rickman and Hutchinson, Architects.

St Peter, Dale End.

All Saints' was the last of the Commissioners' Churches to be built in Birmingham, being opened and consecrated on 28 September 1833. It was designed by Rickman & Hutchinson and provided sittings for 1,200, of which 700 were free, and was built at a cost of £3,817. When built, it was a rectangular building, but a shallow chancel was added in 1881. There were galleries to three sides but these were later removed. A parish was assigned out of St Martin in 1834. It was demolished in the early 1970s.

All Saints', All Saints' Street.

St Michael and All Angels, Field Lane, Bartley Green. This church was built in 1838 by Isaac Newry in a simple Gothic style, in red brick with sandstone dressings. The building was enlarged in 1876 to north-west and south-west to form a T-shaped plan. The church was consecrated in 1840, was a chapel of ease to St Laurence until 1933 when it became a chapel of ease to St Gabriel, Selly Oak, and finally became a parish in 1956. It was replaced by a new church in 1967.

St Michael and All Angels.

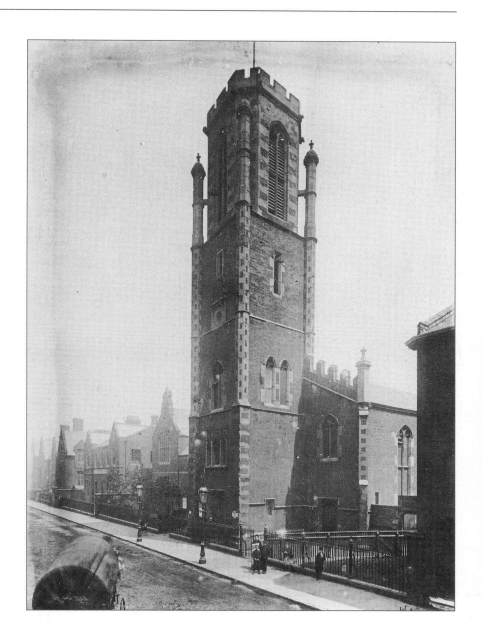

Bishop Ryder
Memorial
Church.

Bishop Ryder Memorial Church, Gem Street. This church was named after Dr
Ryder, the then Bishop of Lichfield, in recognition of help he gave in enabling this
project to start and come to fruition. The foundation stone was laid on 23 August
1837, the church was consecrated on 12 August 1838 and a parish was assigned out
of St Martin in 1841.

Thomas Rickman had a new partner, R.C. Hussey, by this time and the church
was designed by the practice of Rickman & Hussey. It was built in red brick and
sandstone in the Gothic style, the main feature being the west tower standing in
front of the castellated gable of the nave. The chancel was rebuilt in 1894 by J.A.
Chatwin and the building was demolished in 1960.

St Luke, Bristol Street.

St Luke's Church was the third of five churches erected by the Birmingham Church Building Society, although the original intention had been to build ten. The building was designed by Harvey Eggington of Worcester in the Norman style and the cost was £3,700, typical of the cost of these churches and much lower than the cost of the churches built earlier in the century. It was consecrated on 28 September 1842 and a parish was assigned out of St Martin in 1843. The building was condemned as unsafe and demolished in 1899. A new church was built to take its place, which was consecrated in 1903, and which has recently been replaced by a new church in Great Colmore Street.

St Stephen's Church was the fourth of the churches provided by the Birmingham Church Building Society. The building, designed in an Early English style by R.C. Carpenter, cost £3,000, which was given by the governors of King Edward's School. The church was consecrated on 23 July 1844 and a parish was assigned out of St George in the same year. It was a cruciform building, faced in sandstone, and contained chancel, nave, aisles, transepts and small turret. There was extensive rebuilding in 1896 and 1910, the latter, I believe, carried out by W.H. Bidlake. The church closed in 1950.

St Stephen's, Newtown Row.

St Matthias, Farm Street/Wheeler Street, Lozells. The church was a brick building with stone dressings in the Decorated style, by J.L. Pedley, and comprised chancel, nave, aisles and north and south chapels. There was a turret at the west end with a belfry and spire. The church was consecrated on 4 June 1856, assigned a parish out of St George in 1856, closed in 1948 and was subsequently demolished.

Above: St Matthias's Church.
Left: St John the Baptist, Harborne.

St John the Baptist, St John's Road, Harborne. This church was designed by Yeoville Thomason in 1858 in the Early English style, was built in brick and comprised chancel, nave, aisles and tower with spire. The church was consecrated in 1858 and a parish was assigned out of St Peter in 1859. The building was destroyed by enemy action in 1941 and a new church was built on the site of the church hall in High Street.

St Mary, Aston Road North, Aston. This church, designed by J. Murray, was opened and consecrated in 1863. It was built in brick, with stone dressings, in the Decorated style and contained apsidal chancel, nave, aisles, vestry and west and south porches. In 1882 a large, square entrance tower was built in the north-west corner, terminating with a balustrade, pinnacles and a squat spire. A parish was assigned out of St Peter & St Paul, St Silas and St Matthew in 1864 and the church was demolished in 1971.

St Mary's, Aston.

ROMAN CATHOLIC

St Peter, St Peter's Place. A chapel had been built in Masshouse Lane in 1688 but was demolished by a mob after the Glorious Revolution of the same year brought William and Mary to the throne. Therefore, the chapel of St Peter, erected in 1786, is usually looked on as the forerunner of Roman Catholic church-building in Birmingham. The chapel was enlarged in 1802 and 1825, thoroughly repaired in 1871, consecrated in 1933 and demolished in 1969. The plain, red brick building with Gothic windows and scanty stone dressings was deliberately unassuming in appearance to avoid drawing attention to itself and its function. The building comprised a rectangular hall, with a gallery around three sides, and an apsidal chancel.

St Peter's.

St Catherine of Siena, Horsefair

St Catherine of Siena, Horsefair. A mission was established in 1858, firstly in a room over a stable in Bristol Street and then in the upper room of a school in Windmill Street. The permanent church was opened in 1875, designed by Dunn & Hansom, comprising a five-bay nave and wide aisles and the building was faced in red brick with stone dressings. The chancel, ambulatory and south chapel were added in 1893 by Cossins & Peacock. A north-west tower with octagonal belfry and squat, stone spire was added in 1909. The church was demolished in the early 1960s and a replacement was built on the corner of Bristol Street and Irving Street.

BAPTIST

Cannon Street Baptist Church is looked upon as the 'Mother Church' of Birmingham Baptists and was founded in 1737 by a group of local Baptists who had formed part of a church at Bromsgrove. The chapel was built on land forming part of Guest's cherry orchard in 1738. By 1754 congregation numbers were down to fourteen. Things improved after that, helped, presumably, by members joining from Freeman Street, and extensions were made to the chapel in 1763 and 1780. This building was replaced in 1806 by the one illustrated below. This was a square chapel of red brick, the front having a central, pedimented bay, with two round-headed windows above a recessed entrance and stone Tuscan columns. To each side there were narrower bays, slightly recessed, each with one round-headed window at the upper and lower levels. Internally, there were galleries to three sides. The chapel was closed due to the Birmingham Improvement Scheme leading to the construction of Corporation Street, and the congregation moved to the Mount Zion Chapel, Graham Street, in 1880.

Cannon Street Baptist Church, 1874.

Interior and exterior photographs of the Graham Street Chapel.

Mount Zion Chapel opened in 1824 as St Andrew's Presbyterian Church, but in 1827 it became a Baptist chapel. The membership flourished from 1844 when George Dawson became minister but decreased when he left and started the Church of the Saviour in Edward Street in 1846. Most of the congregation moved to Hagley Road after it was built but the original Cannon Street members stayed until 1913 when it closed and was demolished. The congregation founded Spring Hill in 1853 but a chapel was not built until 1886. Mount Zion chapel had a gallery and seating for about 2,000.

Wycliffe Baptist Church was opened in 1861, having been built on a site given by W. Middlemore. The church, built at a cost of £5,965, was designed by James Cranston and built of brick and stone. The accommodation comprised chapel, three vestries, library, two schoolrooms and usual offices. There were galleries to three sides of the chapel. The church was responsible for a mission in Hope Street in 1892. It closed in 1961 and the building was demolished.

The Church of the Redeemer was built in 1881–2 on a site given by W. Middlemore and provided seating for 1,000. The building was designed by James Cubitt of London in a thirteenth-century style, and was built in stone and cruciform in plan. The original membership came mainly from Mount Zion Chapel, who continued with their mission work at Ellen Street and Carter's Lane. The church was demolished in the 1970s but the name lives on in its successor in Monument Road.

Wycliffe Baptist Church, Bristol Street.

Church of the Redeemer, Hagley Road, Edgbaston.

METHODISTS

Cherry Street Chapel was the first to be built in Birmingham by the Wesleyans, was opened by John Wesley in 1782 and was built at a cost of £1,200. It was replaced in 1823 by a new, large, plain brick building with a low-pitched, hipped roof. The chapel, internally, had a continuous gallery. The last sermon in the building was preached on 27 June 1886 by Dr Melsom who had joined the chapel in 1825. The building was demolished in the next month, prior to the congregation moving to the new Central Hall in Corporation Street on the corner of Lower Priory.

Cherry Street Chapel.

St Martin's Street, Islington.

St Martin's Street, Islington. The first chapel was built by the Wesleyan Methodists in 1825 and enlarged in 1840 to provide seating for 898. The church had originated in meetings held in the house of William Ford in William Street in 1817 and then moved to a small chapel on the corner of St Martin's Street and Tennant Street. Another preaching room was used from 1819 to 1825 in Worton Terrace, Lower St Martin's Street. In 1864 a new chapel was added at a cost of £8,658, designed by John Henry Chamberlain, and built to the right of the earlier building. It was built of brick, with stone dressings.

There were extensive alterations to this later building in 1917 and in 1940 it was one of the largest chapels in Birmingham, with seating for 1,200.

Nechells Park Road. The first chapel was built by the Wesleyans in 1837 following cottage meetings which had been held, from 1821 onwards, in Saltley. This building was replaced in 1863 by the building shown here, designed by William Jenkins and seating 700.

This chapel was built of brick with stone and concrete dressings and had an Italianate front attached to it, which looked as though it had been designed for another building, but, as it happened to fit, was used here. The building was declared unsafe in 1929 and a new chapel was built, costing £16,758, designed by A.L. Snow and seating 720.

Nechells Park Road.

The Parade, Sutton Coldfield. This Wesleyan chapel, built on the corner of Newhall Street in 1888, had an entrance lobby, four-bay nave, aisles and an apsidal chancel as well as school rooms under the last three bays of the nave, approached from Newhall Street near the rear of this sloping site. A new chapel was built in South Parade in 1936 to replace this building which became Sutton Coldfield's Central Library until 1974 when it was replaced by a purpose-built library, and this building was demolished and the site redeveloped.

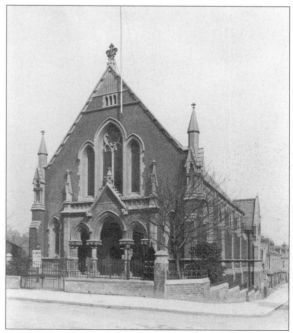

The Parade, Sutton Coldfield.
(Supplied by Sutton Coldfield Reference Library)

UNITED REFORM

Carr's Lane Chapel. The 'Mother Chapel' of Birmingham Congregationalists was founded in 1748 by a secession from the Unitarian Old Meeting. The first building, on a site between Carr's Lane and New Meeting Street, provided seating for 450 but was shut in on all sides by other buildings. It was replaced in 1802 by a new chapel described as 'cold, comfortless and somewhat repulsive in appearance.' The name of the architect is not given. Galleries were added in 1812 but the building was too small for its purpose and a new chapel was built on an extended site, giving seating for 1,800. Thomas Whitwell was happy to have his name mentioned as the architect of the new building, illustrated here, the foundation stone of which was laid on 31 July 1818. The opening of the new building took place on 30 August 1820. In 1876 a new brick front was added, designed by Yeoville Thomason and built in a Renaissance style, also shown here. The church was directly responsible for the establishment of chapels at Wheeler Street, Garrison Lane, Palmer Street, Rushall Lane, Yardley and others outside Birmingham. For a period of over ninety years the church had only two ministers; J.A. James from 1805 to 1859 and he was joined in 1854 by Dr R.W. Dale, who was minister until 1895. Both contributed greatly to the church and, particularly in the case of Dr Dale, to the town and city. The 1820 church was replaced in the late 1960s by a new church, designed by Professor Denys Hinton.

Carr's Lane Chapel – the 1820s building.

Carr's Lane Chapel after the 1876 alterations.

Ebenezer Chapel was built by the congregation at Livery Street in 1818 and the first service was held in December. It was, despite the small drawing of the entrance elevation, a large building, seating 1,600. There was a Sunday School building at the rear and almshouses along each side. The chapel closed in 1929 and the site was sold.

Ebenezer Chapel,
Steelhouse Lane

The interior of Ebenezer Chapel, Steelhouse Lane.

Francis Road, Edgbaston.

Francis Road, Edgbaston. On 11 September 1855 the foundation stone of this chapel was laid and it opened in 1856, having been built at a cost of £5,000. It had been designed by Yeoville Thomason in an Early English style to accommodate 1,000 and was built in stone. The church was cruciform in plan and alterations and extensions took place at the east end in 1892–3. The church was responsible for missions in Sherborne Street in 1871, Wood Street in 1876 (which I know nothing about) and Dartmouth Road in 1902.

Soho Hill, Handsworth.

Soho Hill Chapel was built in 1879 as a continuation of Graham Street Chapel at a cost, including the site, of about £17,000, and provided sittings for 1,000. It was designed by J.H. Fleming in a Lombardic style, was built in facing bricks with stone dressings, and had a long frontage to Soho Hill. The chapel was sold to Joseph Lucas Ltd. in 1941 for £10,500 and the last service was held in the chapel on 28 September 1941. Services were then held at the Gibson Road Unitarian Chapel until Elmwood Chapel at 45 Hamstead Hill opened in 1946 and is still in use.

UNITARIAN

Old Meeting House was registered as a dissenters' chapel in 1689, was severely damaged in the riots of 1715 and burnt down in the riots of 1791. It was a rectangular building with four small gables to the front, each having a rectangular window at the upper level, with pediment-headed doors under the outer windows. A new brick chapel was built to replace it, opening in 1795. The property was sold to the L&NWR in 1881 for £30,000 in connection with the further development of New Street station. Much of this money was used for the building of a replacement chapel in Bristol Street. A prominent feature of the Old Meeting House site was the graveyard, serving both Old and New Meetings, which was enlarged in 1779, 1869 and 1870.

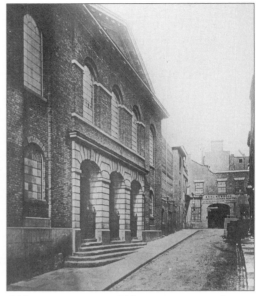

Old Meeting House, Old Meeting House Street.

New Meeting House, Moor Street. Lower Meeting congregation was in existence by 1690, meeting in a building in Deritend that suffered damage in the riots of 1715. A new site was bought in 1727 in Moor Street and the New Meeting House was opened there in 1732. This building was destroyed by fire in the riots of 1791 and the illustration shows the building afterwards. Another chapel was built and opened in 1802 and this continued in use until 1862 when it was sold to the Roman Catholic Church and is still in use as St Michael's Church.

New Meeting House, Moor Street.

The Church of the Saviour was opened by George Dawson, one of Birmingham's most important citizens and proponent of 'the Civic Gospel', in 1847, after he left Mount Zion Baptist Church. He and his successors conducted it as an independent Unitarian chapel until its closure at the end of 1895. The building was designed by Bateman & Drury with seating for 1,400. It was built of brick, with a semi-circular end and an impressive stucco front with the tall central feature crowned with a pediment. Following its closure, the building was occupied by the Primitive Methodists until 1909, then became a variety theatre and ended its career as the Lyric cinema between 1919 and 1960.

Church of the Saviour, Edward Street.

The Church of the Messiah was designed by J.J. Bateman and built in 1862 to replace the New Meeting Chapel in Moor Street. It was designed in the Decorated style and was built over the canal, supported on arches. Many prominent Birmingham families, including the Chamberlains, Kenricks and Nettlefolds worshipped at this church and the minister at that time, Dr H. W. Crosskey, was a great supporter of 'the Civic Gospel'. The church was demolished in 1978.

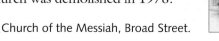

Church of the Messiah, Broad Street.

FRIENDS

Bull Street Meeting House was built in 1703, to replace the one in Newhall Lane erected in 1689. It was a simple brick, rectangular building, built up to the pavement line and was enlarged in 1778 and 1792. It provided seating for 372. In 1857, a new Meeting House was built, set well back from the street, built in red brick with stone dressings, and was designed by T. Plevins. This new building seated 340 at the main level and another 160 at gallery level. This building was replaced in 1931 by the present building and for two years the members met in premises in Upper Priory.

Meeting House,
Bull Street – the 1703
building.

The 1857
building.

SIX

Residential Buildings

The selection is quite varied and not what I expected when I started, for I thought there would be several single detached houses included and, as you will see, I have failed miserably. I have not tried to group the types, as there is not enough of each, and have dealt with them in order of erection.

Four Oaks Hall was built at approximately the time when the seventeenth century gave way, graciously, to the eighteenth century. It was built by the 3rd Lord Ffolliot of Billyshannon and was designed by William Wilson. Over time, it had several owners, but in the 1870s the then owner, Sir John Hartopp, sold the estate of 246 acres to a race course company. The course opened in 1881 but was not successful and was sold in August 1890, together with Four Oaks Park. A royal show was held on part of the estate in 1898 which was visited by the Prince of Wales, after lunch at Four Oaks Hall. The hall, which by now was in a state of decline, was demolished shortly after the show and development of the Four Oaks Estate, which had commenced after the sale in 1890, continued.

Four Oaks Hall, Four Oaks, Sutton Coldfield. *(Supplied by Sutton Coldfield Reference Library)*

Old Square was built on a portion of the old priory land purchased by John Pemberton, the brother-in-law of Sampson Lloyd, in 1697. The houses were designed by William Westley and built by Thomas Kempsey and were sold leasehold. Many prominent citizens lived in the square including Edmund Hector, best remembered for his friendship with Samuel Johnson who often stayed with him. Nos 3 and 4 were converted at the end of the eighteenth century and became the Stork Hotel. The end of Old Square was hastened by the Birmingham Improvement Scheme, resulting in the construction of Corporation Street, which reached Old Square in January 1882 as it passed through in a northerly direction. The last houses were demolished in 1886.

Two views of Old Square; the lower image showing Edmund Hector's house.

Lench's Trust, Steelhouse Lane.

Lench's Trust was established by William Lench in a deed of 1525 and it still exists today. It is best known for the almshouses it has provided, including the development in Steelhouse Lane, carried out in 1764, and providing forty-two rooms. The almshouses were on part of the site later to be occupied by the General Hospital in 1897. The trust did not wait to be asked to move and left in the early 1880s.

The Crescent, first proposed in November 1788 with Charles Norton as developer and John Rawsthorne as architect, was to consist of twenty-three houses of stone in a terrace, 1,182ft long and 17ft high. The centre part was to be 622ft and each wing 140ft, exclusive of a return towards Cambridge Street of another 141ft. The houses would be 'commanding an extensive prospect that cannot ever be interrupted by other buildings'. Twelve houses were completed, mainly in the wings, and then there was a halt, caused by the ruinous war with France, and the halt became a full stop. The houses that were built remained for a long time, long after the view was interrupted by other buildings. The Crescent Theatre occupied one of the buildings, not moving out until 1964. I should point out that the illustration gives a better idea of what was proposed than what was built.

The Crescent.

Bishop's House, Bath Street.

The Bishop's House, on the corner of Bath Street and Weaman Street, was built on the opposite side of the street to St Chad's Cathedral which it was built to serve, providing living accommodation for the bishop and clergy and providing facilities for the transaction of the business of the district. It was built at the same time as the cathedral by the same architect, A.W. Pugin, using the same bricks and with the same austere and impressive appearance. This was one of several important buildings that had the effrontery to stand in the way of the Inner Ring Road.

Josiah Mason's Orphanage. The foundation stone of the orphanage building, designed by J.R. Botham, was laid by Josiah Mason on 19 September 1860 and the building was completed and opened in 1868 having cost £60,000 to build. Josiah Mason not only paid this, but provided endowments of a value of £200,000 to support the orphanage. A management committee consisting of the founder and seven trustees was set up in 1869 and a deed was drawn up stating that on Mason's death an additional seven trustees were to be appointed by the town council.

In 1874 a separate wing was built consisting of dormitories and a schoolroom for 150 boys, connected to the main building by a dining hall capable of seating 500 diners. The orphanage could now accommodate 300 girls, 150 boys and 50 infants. When Josiah Mason died in 1881 he was buried in the mortuary chapel and two

Josiah Mason's Orphanage, Orphanage Road, Erdington, 1908.

years before the buildings were demolished in 1973–4, his remains, together with those of his wife and fifty-four orphanage children, were exhumed and cremated at Perry Barr Crematorium.

Whetstone, Somerset Road, Edgbaston. This, judging from the photograph, rather formidable and forbidding dwelling, was designed by the architect John Henry Chamberlain in 1878 as his own residence. He did not have long to enjoy it, for he died in 1883, but the house remained until the 1960s, when it was demolished to make way for Whetstone Close.

Whetstone.

Princess Alice Orphanage, New Oscott.

Princess Alice Orphanage was a branch of the National Children's Home which had been started in 1869 by Dr Thomas Stephenson, a Wesleyan Methodist. The home was named after Queen Victoria's daughter who had recently died aged thirty-seven. The building was helped by a donation of £10,000, given by Solomon Jeavis. The foundation stone of the first building was laid in 1882 and J.L. Ball designed the administration building in 1884.

The home was very different from Josiah Mason's Orphanage and the children lived in houses spread around the site. While looking for other building applications I have noticed the following applications made by Ball: 1891 Hospital; 1891 School, Seymour House and Outbuilding; 1894 House; 1905 Two Houses; 1906 Out Offices.

The practice of Crouch, Butler & Savage picked up the gauntlet after the First World War and made these applications: 1923 Hospital; 1924 Workshops and School Hall; 1924 Swimming Baths; 1929 Assistant Governor's House; 1932 Memorial Hall. There are almost certainly other applications. All of the buildings have now been demolished, the last being the Clock Tower in October 2000, and the site is now occupied by retail buildings, notably Tesco.

Lawrence Street houses. The first houses built by the council in Birmingham were erected in Ryder Street in 1889. There were twenty-two in number and they were designed by Martin & Chamberlain. Two years later, on land very nearby in Lawrence Street, the council built eighty-two houses. These dwellings, designed by A.H. Davis, were built in terraces of eight at right angles to the street. Except for a development of two-storey flats built in Milk Street near the end of the century,

Houses, Lawrence Street.

these were the only new buildings built by the council for many years and both developments were demolished in 1971 to make way for Aston University.

St Anne's Vicarage, 84 Cato Street, Duddeston. St Anne's Church in Cato Street, designed by J.G. Dunn, was consecrated on 22 October 1869 and closed in 1951. No. 84 Cato Street was built in the latter part of the nineteenth century as a private dwelling but was rebuilt in 1908 to the design of W.H. Bidlake and reopened as the vicarage of St Anne's. After the church closed it became the vicarage of St Matthew's until the mid-1960s when it was demolished.

St Anne's Vicarage, 84 Cato Street, Duddeston.

SEVEN

Hotels & Public Houses

I have put these two categories together because, while it is normally no problem to differentiate between them, there are occasions when the difference between the two is blurred, notably when the word 'hotel' is added to the name of an establishment, presumably because there are bedrooms to let, and yet the main activity of the business is to function as a public house.

HOTELS

Dingley's Hotel, on the corner of New Meeting Street, was built in the reign of King George II and was a fine example of Georgian architecture. It was another victim of the Inner Ring Road, closing in the early 1960s.

Dingley's Hotel,
124 Moor Street,
1905.

Hen & Chickens Hotel, 130 New Street.

The Hen & Chickens originated as an inn in High Street but transferred to a new building in High Street in 1798 and became a hotel, although still retaining many of the characteristics of a coaching inn. The building, which had been designed by James Wyatt, had a portico added to it in 1830, befitting its status. The premises, together with four shops and a piece of land in Worcester Street at the back of the hotel, were purchased to build a new school for King Edward VI High School for Girls, and the hotel was demolished at the beginning of 1895.

The new school was built on the land at the rear, with an entrance to New Street positioned between the Boys' School and the new Hen & Chickens Hotel. The school and the hotel were designed by J.A. Chatwin & Son. The school was opened on 6 November 1896 and the hotel in 1898. After extensions and alterations in 1938 the name was changed to the Arden Hotel, a more sober title, which seemed appropriate for a temperance hotel. The hotel closed in September 1972 and the site was redeveloped.

Queen's Hotel, Stephenson Street.

The Queen's Hotel, designed by William Livlock, which formed the front to New Street station on the Stephenson Street side, opened in June 1854 – the same year as the station. The hotel had sixty bed and dressing room suites, first- and second-class refreshment rooms, large coffee room and smoking room and, although not mentioned, I am sure there were adequate sanitary facilities. The name was changed to North Western (Queen's) Hotel in 1872 to forestall a rival hotelier, but it was changed back at a later time when, presumably, the name would have lost its significance. The hotel was enlarged in 1911 and a new wing added in 1917 and closed in the 1960s when the station was redeveloped.

Great Western Hotel, Colmore Row. This very attractive building, designed by J.A. Chatwin, opened in 1863 in front of Snow Hill station, which had opened in 1852, with temporary structures that were not replaced until 1871. A decision was taken early in the twentieth century to rebuild the station and it was decided that this would be facilitated if the hotel was incorporated into the station, as its trade was decreasing, and the building would be useful for administration offices.

It was closed in 1905, except for the dining room, so that it could be used during the rebuilding of the station which took place between 1906 and 1912. The work included making an access from Colmore Row through the hotel building into the new booking hall which became the principal entrance to the station. The old hotel

Great Western Hotel, Colmore Row, 1890.

building was demolished in 1970, two years before the station closed, having served the purpose for which it was built for well under half of its existence.

Cobden Hotel, 53–7 Corporation Street. This building, dating from 1882, was erected by the Birmingham Coffee House Company and housed the Cobden Temperance Hotel. The architect was William Doubleday and the Gothic style of this building was a great contrast with the Classical style of the Staffordshire Bank in Temple Row, mentioned earlier, but both were a great loss to the city. I have seen two perspectives of this building, with different details to the ground floor of the Cherry Street frontage and hope I have selected the right one, but have no idea if I have. The building was demolished in the late 1950s to make way for Rackham's and the Cobden Hotel moved to Edgbaston.

Cobden Hotel, Corporation Street.

Colonnade Hotel, 95 New Street, 1900.

The Colonnade Hotel, on the corner of Ethel Street, designed by W.H. Ward and erected in 1882, was another building that fulfilled its original, primary function for under half of its existence. The building contained shops, offices, the Midland Conservative Club and the Birmingham Musical Society at varying times, while the hotel kept itself to itself on the upper floors, although this was not enough to stop its closure in 1916. The building was then taken over by the Chamber of Commerce until 1961, when the Chamber moved to its new building in Edgbaston and the old hotel building was demolished.

The Stork Hotel, Corporation Street. I have never seen a street number assigned to this very fine French Renaissance-style building, on the corner of Lower Priory, but assume, if it had lowered itself to use one, it would have been 118–?. The building was designed by W.H. Ward and opened in 1883 and, unlike some other hotels I know (or know of), it stayed as a hotel with the same name for the whole of its existence, which ended when the scourge of good buildings, the Inner Ring Road, found it in its way.

The Stork Hotel, Corporation Street, 1883.

The Woolpack Hotel was built in 1883 and was designed by W.H. Ward who seems to have been very busy designing hotels in 1882–3. The building, as usual with Ward, was built of stone, and the photograph, taken near the end of its days, does not show it as it once was. If you look at the photograph earlier in the book (page 28) of the Public Office, which was next door to the Woolpack, you will see that, at some time, the Woolpack lost its top storey. The building disappeared altogether in the 1950s.

Woolpack Hotel, 8 and 9 Moor Street, 1949.

PUBLIC HOUSES

The Bell occupied a prominent position at the junction with Great Colmore Street, and James & Lister Lea did its best to make sure there was a lot to see, if not much to admire, in this building, erected in 1886–7. It closed on 10 June 1965, after receiving a compulsory purchase order to allow space for road-widening.

The Bell, 57 and 59 Bristol Street.

The Dolphin was built on the Warwick Road between Victoria Road and Dolphin Lane and opened on 16 May 1930. It replaced an old coaching inn but lasted only until 1992 when it was replaced by a supermarket. Freda Cocks, Lord Mayor of Birmingham in 1977–8, was licensee for some years until 1973.

The Dolphin, 1203 Warwick Road, Acocks Green.

The Fox Hollies, situated on the corner of Fox Hollies Road, was opened on 21 September 1928, having received the license of the St Vincent Arms, Ladywood. The building was designed by Edwin F. Reynolds of Wood, Kendrick & Reynolds and closed in 1997 to make way for a supermarket.

The Fox Hollies, Olton Boulevard East, Acocks Green.

Hope & Anchor, Edmund Street.

The Hope & Anchor occupied a position of some importance, being next door to the Birmingham Central Library, almost opposite Sir Josiah Mason's College (later Birmingham University) and just round the corner from the Town Hall. This may give the impression that this pub had pretensions above its class, but that is not true, for the three buildings mentioned chose sites close to the Hope & Anchor and, I think, with three cases, this cannot have been accidental. The Hope & Anchor had been on this site, in Harlow Street as it was then known, since 1763. It was run by the Fletcher family for over one hundred years, the best remembered being former Alderman Eli Fletcher, who was in charge for thirty-four years. The pub was taken over by Ansells, who retained the inside but had the front remodelled by C.J. Hodson in 1893. It closed on 27 June 1965 and was demolished to allow for the redevelopment of the area.

The Longbridge, 1836 Bristol Road South, Rednal.

The Longbridge, situated on the corner of Ashill Road, was designed by S.N. Cooke. It opened on 4 March 1932 and closed on 14 December 1995 to make way for residential development.

The Maypole, on the corner of Maypole Lane, was designed by J. Alfred Harper and opened on 17 July 1936 and closed in 2002 to make way for a supermarket.

Maypole, Alcester Road South, Highter's Heath, 1955.

The Mermaid, Stratford Road, Sparkhill, 1910.

The Mermaid, Sparkhill. Three public houses have stood on this site, at the junction of the important Stratford and Warwick roads. The first was the conversion of a seventeenth-century building into a public house by 1751 or earlier. The second one, shown above, replaced the earlier one in 1895 and I do find it appealing and appropriate for its setting. It was damaged in the Second World War and was rebuilt in 1949.

The Speedwell, 225 Stockfield Road, South Yardley. It is hard to imagine that this restrained, brick-built public house on the corner of Amington Road was built within a year of the black-and-white timbered Black Horse public house, Northfield, and was designed by the same architectural practice, Bateman & Bateman. The Speedwell opened on 18 January 1929 and its license was surrendered on 24 May 1991. The site was subsequently occupied by a car showroom.

The Speedwell, South Yardley, 1930.

White Horse, 30 Congreve Street.

White Horse, 30 Congreve Street. This impressive building was referred to as the White Horse Hotel but I always thought of it as a mixture of public house and restaurant, the latter part possibly influenced by the fact that the Swiss-born chef at the establishment was the husband of a friend of my mother.

The building was designed by Wood & Kendrick and built in 1906, at a cost of £17,484. It was a popular meeting place and its closure, on 30 June 1965, was a sad loss.

The Woodman existed as a tavern from 1820 but it is remembered now from 1850 onwards, when it was bought by James Onions and the controlling group of the Town Council, known as the Economists, who met here to discuss business and decide policy. It was also a popular meeting place for theatrical people, particularly those appearing at the Theatre Royal.

The Woodman was rebuilt in 1891 by Henry Naden, not an architect well known by me, but he produced a memorable building, internally and externally. Among the many features that made this building so special were the tiled pictures of Birmingham buildings on the walls of the public bar and the statue of the woodman in his setting, externally. Sadly, the Woodman closed on the last day of 1964 to make way for Paradise Circus and a building that was unique was lost.

The Woodman,
5 Easy Row,
6 June 1952.

Yew Tree, Church Road/Stoney Lane, Yardley.

The Yew Tree Inn was opened on 22 January 1926, being one of the superior type of pub that was built in the suburbs between the wars. It was designed by James & Lister Lea, a firm that had designed more public houses in Birmingham than any other practice. The Yew Tree closed on 26 July 2000, later to be replaced by shops.

Two books I have found very useful and will tell you much more about pubs are *'Time Please!'* by Andrew Maxam and *Birmingham Pubs* by Keith Turner.

EIGHT

Places of Entertainment

THEATRES

I have not been able to find illustrations of some of the theatres and, in other cases, have found illustrations after they were converted to cinemas, in which case they will be covered in that section hence the selection under this heading is limited.

Theatre Royal, New Street. This theatre, known originally as the New Theatre and designed by Samuel Wyatt, opened on 20 June 1774. It was severely damaged by fire on 17 August 1792, was rebuilt to the design of George Sanders, and reopened on 22 June 1795. The name was changed to the Theatre Royal on 1 August 1807 and, at that time, the theatre was open for only four months of the year, between June and September. Another fire occurred in January 1820 and the theatre reopened on Monday 14 August 1820, the rebuilding having been designed by Samuel Beazley. The frontage, to New Street, was not affected by either fire.

The theatre was closed after the performance of *David Garrick* on 4 January 1902, demolished and rebuilt, the architects being Runtz & Ford. The new theatre,

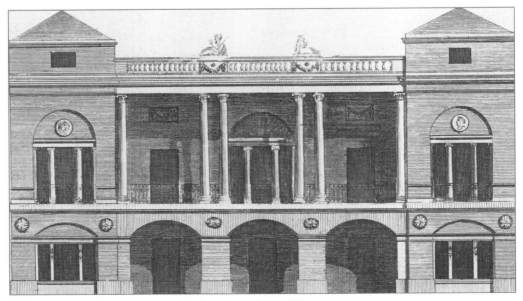

Theatre Royal, New Street, in a drawing dating from 1788.

with a seating capacity of 2,200 and built at a cost of £50,000, opened on 16 December 1904 with a performance of the pantomime, *Babes in the Wood*. It closed finally on 15 December 1956 and was demolished, being replaced by the Woolworth Building, a poor exchange.

Holder's Concert Hall, Coleshill Street. Henry Holder, the owner/licensee of the Rodney Inn, opened a concert hall adjacent to the inn, at 87 Coleshill Street, in 1843. It was extended in 1846 and 1857 and after the last extension could accommodate 2,000.

It had several changes of name, becoming the Birmingham Concert Hall in 1871, the Gaiety Concert Hall in 1886 and the Gaiety Theatre of Varieties in 1897, all following changes of ownership. In its later years it occasionally showed films and closed as a music hall in 1920 and was converted to a cinema, known as the Gaiety. It was extensively damaged in 1936 and, after rebuilding, reopened in December 1939. The rebuilt cinema had an austere symmetrical, brick-faced front, with a horizontal band of 1930s-style windows situated above the central canopy. It was designed by C.J. Foster, the ABC architect.

Holder's Concert Hall, Coleshill Street, 1855.

Prince of Wales, Broad Street.

Prince of Wales, Broad Street. The theatre was opened on 3 September 1856 having been built at a cost of £12,000, and was known then as the Birmingham Music Hall. Charles Dickens gave a reading of *A Christmas Carol* at the theatre in 1861 and the name of the theatre was changed in 1862, after the building was sold, to Prince of Wales Operetta House, although the last two words of the title were dropped in 1865.

The theatre was virtually destroyed in a bombing raid in April 1941 and the remainder was demolished in 1987 to make way for the International Convention Centre and Symphony Hall.

I can remember going to see Arthur Askey and Billy Bennett in the pantomime, *Jack and Jill*, in the 1937/8 season.

The Grand Theatre opened on 14 November 1883, having been designed by W.H. Ward. It had stalls, two circles, gallery and eight boxes, providing seating for 2,200.

It was bought by Moss Empires in 1907 and the interior was redesigned. It continued as a theatre until 1930 and was then used as a cinema from September 1930 until May 1933. It then became the Grand Casino Ballroom, which is how I remember it, although I never went there.

It closed in 1960 to allow for redevelopment.

Grand Theatre, Corporation Street, 1890.

Imperial Theatre, High Street, Bordesley.

Imperial Theatre. A building application was submitted for this theatre in March 1898 by Owen & Ward on behalf of C.E. Machin and J. Bacon, and it opened on 2 October 1899 having cost £25,000 to build. It was taken over by Moss Empires in 1903, was refurbished and changed its name to Bordesley Palace. It closed as a theatre in 1929 and reopened as a cinema. It was taken over by the Ministry of Food during the Second World War to be used as a food store. It was demolished in 1957.

Carlton Theatre, Vauxhall. This theatre, on the corner of Nechells Place, opened on 16 July 1900, cost £14,000 to build, consisted of stalls, dress circle, gallery and six boxes, and the architect was Thomas Guest. Its name was changed to Birmingham Coliseum and Gaiety in 1911 and closed as a theatre in 1921. It then became the Coliseum Cinema, but was destroyed in an air raid in 1941.

Carlton Theatre, Saltley Road, Vauxhall.

Aston Hippodrome, Potter's Lane, Aston.

Aston Hippodrome was designed by James & Lister Lea, a practice better known for the design of public houses with its masterpiece, the Barton Arms very close to this theatre.

The building, erected at a cost of £10,000, opened on 7 December 1908 and was destroyed by fire in February 1938. It was restored at a cost of £30,000 and opened again six months after the fire. It closed as a theatre in June 1960 before later being used as a bingo hall and was demolished in September 1980.

The Aston Theatre Royal is covered by the Astoria cinema in the next section.

CINEMAS

I think that when I was young, the most popular form of entertainment outside of the home was the cinema. Most people living in Birmingham had a choice of cinemas close to home to visit, and most suburban cinemas had three changes of programme each week; Monday to Wednesday, Thursday to Saturday and Sunday. The programme usually comprised an 'A' film, a 'B' film, news and forthcoming attractions and hardly any advertisements. The programmes were continuous and my friends and I would normally go in halfway through the 'B' film and then sit there until it came round again, sometimes staying longer if there was an interesting sequence further on.

As children we could go in on our own to see 'U'-rated films but to see an 'A'-rated film we had to be accompanied by an adult. If our parents were not prepared to take us, we would stand outside and ask strangers to take us in and would almost always find someone prepared to oblige. It must be hard to imagine that today, but I remember those days, and cinema visits, with great fondness.

I am listing the selected buildings in alphabetical order, as I could think of no better arrangement. I feel it would be appropriate, for an old picturegoer, to start with the letter 'N' and wait for it to come around again but, for the benefit of the younger readers, I am going to start at 'A'.

The Alhambra opened on Boxing Day 1928, closed at the end of August 1968, carried on as an Asian cinema for six years and then was demolished. The cinema was designed by Roland Satchwell and Ernest Roberts (the father of James A. Roberts, the architect of the Rotunda and other city centre buildings). The external front was a restrained, symmetrical design, mainly of brick, that bore little

resemblance to the interior. I assume the name was chosen first and influenced the interior, rather than the other way round. The design was Moorish, with domes over the pay box and the exits each side of the proscenium arch. The design was based on the Alhambra in Granada and I know now why I kept thinking of the Moseley Road, when I was in Granada.

Alhambra, Moseley Road.

Actually, this is not entirely true, for I spent the whole time wondering why I was not wearing more as it was so surprisingly cold.

The Alhambra was an important building, being the first atmospheric cinema in Birmingham. I do not think I ever visited it and that would appear to have been my loss.

Astoria, Aston Road North. This was opened in 1893 as the Aston Theatre Royal and was designed by Mr Ward (presumably W.H. Ward, but not one of his best buildings). It became the Astoria cinema in December 1927 and closed as a cinema in November 1955. It was converted to a television studio for ABC and ATV and screened its first show in February 1956. Despite its efforts to stay at the forefront of entertainment the building finally succumbed when ATV moved to new premises in the early 1970s and it was demolished. One unusual feature of the building as a cinema was that due to its original design as a theatre it had to have rear projection, with the projectors positioned about 25ft behind the screen.

Astoria,
Aston Road North.

The Beaufort opened on the fifteenth anniversary of the start of the First World War and I am writing this on the day after the ninetieth anniversary of its commencement. It was designed by Archibald Hurley Robinson, possibly Birmingham's most prolific cinema architect. Chris and Rosemary Clegg described the Beaufort as 'perhaps his greatest achievement', but I wouldn't go further than to describe it as one of his best. Although he designed many cinemas, I don't think there was a recognisable Hurley Robinson style or standard.

Externally, the Beaufort had an imposing entrance, seemingly separated from the lofty auditorium but, presumably, the two connected happily and efficiently. It was described as a Tudor hall, with a convincing atmosphere and, looking at photographs I think it looks more convincing from the screen than from the circle and not very welcoming.

Beaufort, Coleshill Road, Ward End.

The Bristol, Bristol Road, Edgbaston. I think it would be hard to find a building that exemplified the architectural appearance of its decade better than the Bristol. The decade was the 1930s (the building opened in May 1937), the architect was Archibald Hurley Robinson and I think it compares favourably with the Beaufort.

In 1963, the Bristol became Birmingham's only Cinerama cinema, the main purpose of which seemed to be, judging from photographs, to cover the area with garish advertising hoardings and, in 1972, it was altered to accommodate three

Bristol, Bristol Road, Edgbaston.

screens. This ended in 1987 and the building was demolished to make way for a well known restaurant group.

The Broadway opened in 1923, on the site of a former cinema, dating from about 1911. It was designed by Horace G. Bradley and was a neat, formal design, symmetrical, except for some doors at the right end, which, I hope, were added later. From a photograph, it would seem that the programmes were displayed above roof level.

Broadway, Bristol Street.

In 1956 the cinema was altered and became the Cinephone to show foreign films. The frontage was redesigned by H. Werner Rosenthal to give a modern appearance and, whatever I thought at the time, I am now doubtful whether it was for the better. It closed in 1977 and continued as a private cinema, under the names 'Gala' and 'Climax', until 1984, when it reached an anti-climax.

The interior of the Edgbaston, 233–5 Monument Road.

The Edgbaston opened on Christmas Eve 1928 and continued for forty years as a cinema. After that it was a bingo hall for a few years and then was demolished.

It was a large imposing building, designed by Harold S. Scott, of an appearance very popular at the time and instantly recognisable as a cinema.

The Empress cinema, in the centre of Sutton Coldfield, opened on 1 January 1923 and closed in July 1971 after nearly fifty years' continuous service – or it would have been continuous if there had not been closures in 1930 for redecoration and the installation of sound equipment, and in 1935/6 for extensions and alterations.

The Empress, The Parade, Sutton Coldfield.

The building was designed by Satchwell & Roberts and built by W.H. James & Son, who were also the owners, which was probably a good thing, as the cost of the building was expected to be £25,000 and finished at £40,000.

The site is now occupied by shops and the Sutton Coldfield Library, which I visit frequently.

Gaumont Palace, Steelhouse Lane. I think if you had asked any ordinary Birmingham citizen to tell you the name of the cinema in Steelhouse Lane the answer would have been 'the Gaumont', the word 'Palace' occupying the role of a sleeping partner. It was the premier cinema in Birmingham from its opening in February 1931, at least until the opening of the Paramount cinema in New Street in September 1937, and I am not certain that it surrendered its title even then.

The cinema was known for its organ and I have seen the names of organists mentioned, but the name I remember, and possibly it had no connection with the Gaumont, organs or reality, is Felton Rapley.

Gaumont Palace, Steelhouse Lane.

It was also famous for the record-breaking run of 168 weeks, between 1965 and 1968, of *The Sound of Music*. I did go to see it, but thought once was enough, which was not the opinion of everyone.

The cinema had an imposing asymmetrical front, mainly of facing bricks. The architect was William T. Benslyn who, if I remember correctly, was better known as a designer of schools although I could not name any at the moment.

The Kings Norton cinema.

The Kings Norton cinema opened on 16 April 1938, showing the film *Maytime*. It was designed by Harold S. Scott, who designed some of the best and most restrained cinemas in Birmingham. The cinema accommodated 850 in the stalls and 280 in the balcony. It closed on 15 June 1983, with the film *Tootsie,* and the building was subsequently demolished and replaced by a residential development, named Grosvenor Court.

Lozells Picture House, Lozells Road.

Lozells Picture House. This cinema was opened in 1911 but was rebuilt in 1922, the architect being Horace G. Bradley, who designed several cinemas.

It reopened in December 1922 and continued until July 1942 when it was destroyed in an air raid in which the manager, Lionel Jennings, who was on fire-watching duty, was killed.

The Maypole cinema.

The Maypole cinema opened on 1 August 1937, with a George Formby film, *Keep Your Seats Please.* The building was designed by Ernest S. Roberts and was easily recognised as a building from the 1930s. It had seating for 738 in the stalls and 377 in the balcony, but the seats were not occupied for very long, since the cinema was closed on 26 January 1961 after showing the film, *The Lost World.* The building was demolished and replaced by a shopping centre.

The Oak, Bristol Road,
Selly Oak.

The Oak cinema was designed by Harold S. Scott, the father of my last employer. Although I was aware he had designed cinemas, I had not appreciated the high standard he achieved, even if they do give the impression, quite rightly, that the films are to be enjoyed seriously and not frivolously.

The building opened in 1929, was extended in 1935, reopened in December 1935 and closed in November 1979. The building was demolished five years later to allow for road-widening and redevelopment. I pass through Selly Oak only occasionally and have to concentrGaumont Palace, Steelhouse Lane.ate on the altered road layout, but do get the impression the area looked better when the Oak was thriving and there was more of a village atmosphere.

Pavilion, Chester Road, Wylde Green. This was a cinema with an austere and impressive appearance, similar to its twin at Stirchley, both of which were designed by Harold S. Scott. It opened in October 1931 and closed for the showing of films in September 1960. It was converted to a bowling alley but in the 1970s, the ABC Bowl, as it was then known, was demolished and the site is now occupied by houses.

On a personal note, I visited the Pavilion often and it was here, during the Second World War, that I saw *Gone with the Wind*.

Pavilion, Wylde Green.

Regal, 397 Soho Road, Handsworth.

The Regal was the largest suburban cinema and was designed by Harold S. Scott. It opened in October 1929 and closed in November 1968. After this, it was used as a bingo hall and then an Asian cinema before closing again in the late 1970s, to be followed by demolition. It was the first cinema in Birmingham to show talking pictures from its opening.

The Rialto was one of the many cinemas designed by Archibald Hurley Robinson and it had a curved entrance that didn't seem to bear much relationship to the rest of the building. It opened in October 1927 and lasted only until May 1959 and was then demolished and replaced by a supermarket.

Rialto, Stratford Road, Hall Green.

The Robin Hood cinema was designed by Henry E. Farmer and as he was not a prolific designer of cinemas, as far as I know, he obviously decided to let himself go with this one, both internally and externally, and with some success, for it was a well loved cinema.

Its first performance took place on Boxing Day 1927 and closed in March 1970, to be demolished and replaced by a supermarket, for the citizens of Hall Green may love a cinema but believe in getting their priorities right.

Robin Hood, Stratford Road, Hall Green.

I have seen the **Scala** described as a grand luxury cinema. Either my memory must be failing or I used to visit the wrong place for I don't recall getting that impression. It was designed by Essex & Goodman, opened in March 1914 and closed in June 1960 to allow for the new ring road to be built. A new cinema of the same name was built, which opened in November 1964 and was designed by James A. Roberts.

Scala, Smallbrook Street.

Tivoli, Coventry Road, Yardley.

The Tivoli cinema was designed by Satchwell & Roberts and was built side on to the road, giving it a long frontage and an uncommon appearance. It opened in October 1927 and its last performance was shown on 1 July 1961. It was demolished to make way for a shopping centre – which hopefully included a supermarket.

The Tudor was a wide-fronted cinema, designed by Harold S. Scott, which opened on 30 March 1929 and closed on 17 March 1962. After this it was operated as a Social Centre and Bingo Club, before being demolished in the 1990s to make way for housing.

Tudor, Haunch Lane, Yardley Wood.

Victoria, 320 Victoria Road, Aston.

The Victoria. This cinema had an imposing three bay, symmetrical façade, dominated by a central, semi-circular arch containing the entrances, with plenty of space to spare.

The architect was H.W.W. Lovegrove. It opened in December 1924 and closed in August 1963. It was subsequently demolished, but not, as far as I know, to make way for a supermarket.

The West End. Curzon Hall was designed by Edward Holmes in about 1865, approximately the same time as he designed the Masonic Hall in New Street, later to house the Forum. Waller Jeffs was involved with Curzon Hall and showed films, from 1899, as part of his programme of entertainments.

The building was reconstructed in 1924/5, when the canopy was added, by Frederick Pepper and reopened as the West End cinema in March 1925 and continued to show films until March 1967, after which it was demolished.

From October 1948 until February 1952 I worked on the top floor of 83 Suffolk Street, on the corner of Paradise Street, and looked out directly at the

West End, Suffolk Street.

West End cinema, except when I was seated at a drawing board facing Paradise Street.

The building also housed the West End Ballroom, where I went on New Year's Eve 1947, three days after I was demobbed, to meet a young lady I had met once before a few months previously, and who later became my wife.

To find out more about cinemas I suggest you read *The Dream Palaces of Birmingham* by Chris & Rosemary Clegg and *Birmingham Cinemas* by Victor J. Price.

OTHER VENUES

Bingley Hall was erected in 1850 in the grounds of Bingley House, with its main frontage to King Alfred's Place and stretching back to King Edward's Place. It was a large exhibition hall, built by Branson & Chester and designed by a young man in his twentieth year, gaining experience in the office, named Julius Alfred Chatwin. The first large Cattle and Poultry Show in the Midlands had been held in a temporary building in Lower Essex Street in December 1849, and Bingley Hall was opened in time to host the second in December 1850 and continued to hold it annually in the same month for many years. It was used for many events including political meetings, with speakers such as William Gladstone and Joseph Chamberlain, trade shows, dog shows, agricultural shows and the Ideal Home Exhibition, which I can remember visiting. The building was damaged by fire in 1983 and demolished in 1984.

Bingley Hall, King Alfred's Place.

Crystal Palace, Sutton Coldfield. *(Supplied by Sutton Coldfield Reference Library)*

Crystal Palace, Clifton Road, Sutton Coldfield. The Royal Promenade Gardens, comprising 30 acres of land off Clifton Road in the area now occupied by the Youth Centre and the Wyndley Leisure Centre, were opened in 1868 by Job Cole. The gardens, in addition to the planting and walks, had facilities for cricket, croquet, bowls and archery. There was also the opportunity for boating on nearby Wyndley Pool. The complex included a hotel and stabling for horses. The gardens were a great success and in one season there were 110,000 visitors.

The *Sutton Coldfield News*, in its issue of 25 February 1878, announced that the Sutton Coldfield Crystal Palace Company Limited had acquired the Royal Promenade Gardens and Hotel from Mr Cole and would erect a new building comprising a hotel, a winter garden, a skating rink and an aquarium. The new hotel was to be larger than its predecessor with dining rooms capable of seating 600 people. Its façade, facing the park, was to be built in red brick with Bath stone dressings and there would be ornamental towers at each end, the whole roofed with slates. At the rear of the hotel there was to be a large winter garden, available for concerts, public dinners, balls, flower shows and similar purposes. Connected with the winter garden there was to be a long glass building with a large glass dome at the end, 90ft high. The floor was to be covered with asphalt providing a skating surface of 8,000 sq ft. Around the rink and overlooking the gardens there was to be a terrace promenade, 150yds long and under this would be the aquarium. The architect for this project was W.H. Ward and the builder was Horsley Brothers.

In the early years of the First World War, two battalions of the Royal Warwickshire Regiment were stationed in Sutton Park and the headquarters of one was in the Crystal Palace. Pat Collins, the showman, took over the Crystal Palace in the early part of the twentieth century and a fun fair and a miniature railway and these two attractions and the building are all that I can remember. The building was demolished in 1962 and the fun fair closed later in the same year.

The site of the **Aston Lower Grounds** was bounded by Witton Road, Witton Lane, Trinity Road and Bevington Road and covered an area of 31 acres. The site had formed part of the grounds of Aston Hall which had been divided by Trinity Road and the upper part, containing Aston Hall, became Aston Park. H.G. Quilter became the tenant of the neglected Lower Grounds and started a steady development of the site in 1864 and opened it formally to the public in 1872.

The grounds contained a large fish pond, known as Dovehouse Pool. To this was added a cricket ground, later to be bisected by Nelson Road, an adjacent bowling green, grandstands facing the cricket ground and the pool, refreshment room, tobogganing, slide, band pavilion, formal and informal gardens, conservatories and walks.

Aston Lower Grounds, Trinity Road, Aston.

On the other side of Witton Road was the Staffordshire Pool, used for boating. More significant buildings were the Holte Hotel, used as the headquarters and which is still there, and a large complex, built in 1879, containing an aquarium with fine art galleries above, and backed by a skating rink. At right angles to this was the Great Hall, 220ft long by 90ft wide, with galleries on three sides. This building was designed by Thomas Naden and was not finally demolished until August 1981, after the North Stand of Villa Park containing new offices was built. A significant highlight took place after the opening of the site when HRH Prince Arthur opened the Royal Horticultural Society's show on 14 June 1872. The Lower Grounds were used for many sporting events, including cricket, athletics, cycling and football, with Aston Villa winning its first ever trophy, the Birmingham Senior Cup, here in 1880. An agreement was reached in 1896 between Edgar Flower, then the owner of the Lower Grounds, and Aston Villa FC Ltd, for the latter to have a twenty-one-year lease of the site, with an option to buy within that period.

Villa Park. Aston Villa moved to the new site from its ground in Wellington Road called Perry Barr. E.B. Holmes was selected to design the new stadium which included a grandstand along the Witton Lane frontage, with a distinctive barrel roof, which accommodated 10,000, of whom 5,500 were seated. There was terracing around the rest of the ground for another 40,000 standing supporters, with a covered section on the Trinity Road side giving shelter to 8,000. Between the football pitch and the spectators was a cycling track, semi-circular at each end.

Villa Park. The match against Arsenal in 1952 is in progress.

Villa Park, Trinity Road, Aston, 1985.

Thomas Naden's building was used for a gymnasium and offices. The first match was played at the new stadium on Saturday 17 April 1897 against Blackburn Rovers, which Villa won 3–0. Before the First World War, plans were made to build a new grandstand on the Trinity Road side and to alter the terraces. However, the project had to be postponed and the new stand, designed by Archibald Leitch, was not formally opened until 26 January 1924, in a match against Bolton Wanderers, attended by HRH the Duke of York. The Witton Lane stand was replaced in 1963, the Trinity Road stand in 2000 and the ground now bears no resemblance to the original.

NINE

Industrial Buildings

I have not found it easy to make the selection for this section and in some cases I have chosen examples that identify the company and its importance to Birmingham rather than an individual building.

Soho Manufactory. Matthew Boulton, who was born in Birmingham on 3 September 1728, started work in his father's business in Snow Hill in 1749, which manufactured buckles, clasps, chains and other trinkets, and earned himself a good reputation for the quality of his workmanship. The premises in Snow Hill became inadequate for the changes the son wanted to make in the business and in the mid-1750s, in conjunction with his father, Boulton bought Sarehole Mill and Farm. These

A very early photograph of Soho Manufactory.

premises, possibly because of the location, were not ideal and in 1762 he bought a lease, with ninety-four years to run, for land on Handsworth Heath, where the Hockley Brook had been diverted to form a pool to run a water mill for rolling metal. He rebuilt and enlarged the mill, but soon found he needed more space. Therefore, in 1764, he commenced building the Soho Manufactory which was completed in 1765 at a cost of £9,000, and which was capable of accommodating 1,000 workers.

The building consisted of four squares, connected by ranges of workshops and it contained also showrooms and, on the top floor, some living accommodation for workers. At this time, Boulton was in partnership with John Fothergill making larger items such as candelabra and vases and silver and plated wares. Later in the 1780s, part of the manufactory was turned over to the manufacture of coinage, firstly of overseas currencies and trade tokens, but eventually for the Crown. In 1774, Boulton went into partnership with James Watt and in 1796 the Soho Foundry was opened, later to be occupied by W. & T. Avery, the scale manufacturers. The sons of Boulton and Watt eventually took over the business, but it went into a steady decline. The manufactory, at one time the most prestigious industrial building in the world, closed in 1848, after the death of James Watt Jnr. and it was demolished in 1865. The building was the first industrial building to have gas lighting, invented by William Murdock, an employee of the firm, and part of the famous triumvirate, Boulton, Watt & Murdock.

Cadbury Brothers, Bridge Street. John Cadbury was a tea and coffee merchant in Bull Street, who became interested in the marketing of cocoa and set up a cocoa and chocolate factory in Crooked Lane in 1831, where he stayed until 1847 when the

Cadbury Brothers, Bridge Street.

factory was demolished to make way for the Great Western Railway. After a few months at premises in Cambridge Street, the business moved to Bridge Street. In 1849, John, who had been joined in partnership by his brother, Benjamin, gave up the Bull Street business and passed it on to his nephew, Richard Cadbury Barrow. John followed his brother into retirement in 1861 and the business was taken over by his sons, Richard and George. They took over when the firm was in a very depressed state and this continued for some years. Eventually, thanks to their efforts and the support of the workers, things changed for the better and it became necessary to find larger and more convenient premises if progress was to be maintained. A site of 14.5 acres was located at Kings Norton and was bought at auction on 18 June 1878. A start was made on the new factory, designed by George H. Gadd at what was to be called Bournville, in January 1879 and was finished by the autumn. The names Cadbury and Bournville became known throughout the world, but it was at Bridge Street that the great change in the firm's fortunes took place under Richard and George. I know very little about the Bridge Street factory and it was not an architectural gem. I think it is of interest to see an illustration of the factory that led to the creation of Bournville

Bentley & Playfair. A partnership to manufacture guns was made by John Bentley from Birmingham, and Charles Playfair, a Scotsman, in the 1840s and was strengthened by the marriage of Playfair to Bentley's daughter, Louisa. Their first factory was at 56 Summer Lane, between New Summer Street and Lower Tower

Bentley & Playfair, 315–16 Summer Lane.

Street, but a move was made to larger premises on the other side of Summer Lane, at nos 315 and 316, between Brearley Street and Tower Street, in about 1860. By 1883 the address was confined to no. 315 and 316 was occupied by the Revd Frank Henry Weston, the vicar of St Nicolas, and in later years it was used as a Salvation Army lodging house. Bentley & Playfair stayed at Summer Lane until 1911. The firm was then, presumably, taken over by Isaac Hollis, for in 1912 the firm of Hollis, Bentley & Playfair were in business at Hollis's works in Lench Street. As a separate matter, Charles Playfair was on the first board of BSA, set up in 1868.

Globe Works, at its peak, stretched from Gooch Street almost to Lower Essex Street, being frustrated by the Rose & Crown public house which occupied the corner site. John Hawkes began the business of making looking glasses in 1859 although in 1864 the only reference to a looking glass manufacturer in that section of Bromsgrove Street in *Kelly's Directory* was to Chas. Deakin at no. 123, court 7. Obed Charles Hawkes joined his brother in the business which, in 1883, occupied

O.C. Hawkes Limited, Globe Works, Bromsgrove Street.

123–9 Bromsgrove Street. By the turn of the twentieth century, the firm had become O.C. Hawkes Ltd. and now covered nos 121–30. The business also made vacuum cleaners and were electrical sign contractors to the London Underground. The firm continued until the late 1930s but by 1940 only the Rose & Crown remained between Gooch Street and Lower Essex Street.

Birmingham Small Arms Company Limited. Birmingham had been prominent in the small arms trade for centuries before the start of the Crimean War, with many gunsmiths making guns by hand as no suitable machinery existed to improve on the skill of the craftsmen. The need for many more weapons for the war was answered when the government discovered machinery in the United States capable of making guns of equal standard and much more quickly than by hand and installed these in the ordnance factory in Enfield. In order to compete, a group of gunsmiths formed a company in June 1861 and called it Birmingham Small Arms Co. Ltd., to be better known as BSA. The company bought a site off Golden Hillock Lane in Small Heath, comprising 25 acres. A pathway on it was made into a road connecting the site to Golden Hillock Lane and was named Armoury Road. A large, impressive factory, designed by Thomas W. Goodman, was built on the site at a cost of £17,050 and it was completed by 1866. The building was notable for its round-arched windows and its taller, square, corner towers with hipped roofs. Business was good and the first extension was added within five years. The firm played a very important part in the production of weaponry in both world wars, but by then the company was even better known for the production of cycles, motor cycles, cars and many other products. Eventually there were twenty-six companies and four overseas subsidiaries controlled by BSA. The original factory remained but it was dwarfed and obscured by the other buildings on the site and there were many other sites. However things started to go wrong in the 1950s, by which time the production of motor cycles was the main reason for the company's existence, which ended in the 1970s and the original factory was demolished in 1977.

Birmingham Small Arms Company Limited, Armoury Road, Small Heath, 1867.

Samuel Mason set up as a beer machine maker in Dale End, in the section between Moor Street and Chapel Street, in the early 1860s. His address in 1864 was at no. 59 and some years later he was at nos 55 and 56. In the 1880s he moved into a new building at nos 57 and 58, designed for him by Oliver Essex. He had earned a good reputation for the quality of his work and won medals for his beer engines and spirit fountains. Among his rivals was the firm of Gaskell & Chambers, who moved into nos 50–2 in 1894, having taken over the previous owners. Samuel Mason was made bankrupt in 1910 and Gaskell & Chambers took over the bar-fitting business. A new start was made quickly at no. 55, under the name of Harry Mason Ltd., where it remained until the early 1930s. A short move was then made from Dale End to Coleshill Street for a stay of thirty years. Nos 57 and 58 Dale End disappeared in the mid-1950s.

Samuel Mason, 57 and 58 Dale End.

An aerial photograph of Joseph Lucas, Great King Street.

Lucas, Great King Street. Joseph Lucas started to make lamps in 1872 and opened his first factory, in Little King Street, in 1876. He produced a ship's lamp named the 'Tom Bowling' and a cycle lamp known as the 'King of the Road' in the early days, both of which were a great success. Another factory was opened in Great King Street from 1889, which was to become the headquarters of the company and was vastly extended into adjoining streets up until the 1930s. The firm became a public company in 1897, Joseph Lucas & Son Ltd., but Joseph Lucas died five years later. The firm went from strength to strength, with Joseph's son, Harry, and grandson, Oliver, playing a prominent part and the range of electrical products increased enormously. By the time of the centenary, in 1972, there were sixty manufacturing and distributing companies in the group and 100,000 employees. However, a decline set in during the 1980s. Lucas merged with the American company, Varity Corporation in 1996. The merged company was then taken over by TRW in 1999. Before that the Great King Street premises had been closed and the site sold to Birmingham Corporation.

General Electric Co. Ltd., Electric Avenue, Witton.

The General Electric Co. Ltd., better known as the GEC, started in the 1880s in London by Gustav Byng, came to Birmingham in 1896, firstly to a factory in Great Hampton Street and then to Sherlock Street. A site of 110 acres was bought at Witton in 1900 and building work began in the October and was completed in 1902, the buildings covering 45 acres. The photograph of 1930 shows further development and more continued up to 1950, including a heavy engineering works filling in much of the vacant area from Electric Avenue and new buildings on the far side of the canal. All that remains of this once vast complex is the front part of the administration building, erected in the 1920s, to a depth of about 10ft. This building is the light coloured one shown at the end of the open space from Electric Avenue and it forms the frontage to one of the last units to be built on what is now Junction 6 Industrial Park.

If you want to read more about industrial buildings in Birmingham I would recommend two books by Ray Shill, *Workshop of the World – Birmingham's Industrial Legacy* and *Birmingham's Industrial Heritage: 1900–2000*.

TEN

Other Buildings

In this section I have placed buildings that do not easily fit into any of the previous categories or could fit into more than one.

Gosta Green Market Hall was erected in 1837 and occupied an island site, bounded by AB Row, Belmont Row and Prospect Row. The house at the front was the residence of the market superintendent. I do not know for how long it continued as a market hall; it appeared in a directory of 1847 as such but had no mention in a directory of 1852 and later references were to the Old Market Hall in brackets. I have seen a copy of an O.S. map of the early twentieth century, showing the isolated site covered by the words 'Old Market Hall'. I think the building had several occupants and was demolished not long after the photograph above was taken.

Market Hall, Gosta Green, 18 June 1963.

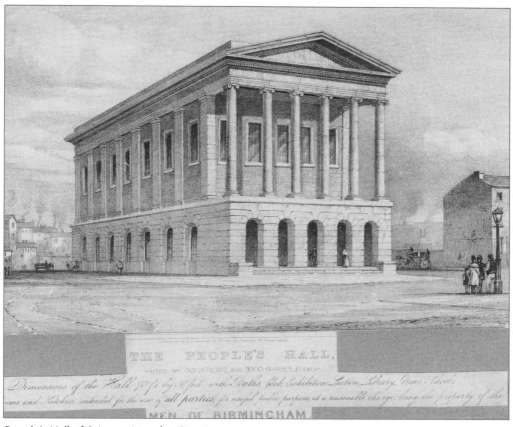

People's Hall of Science, Loveday Street.

People's Hall of Science. I came across this fascinating illustration when I was looking, unsuccessfully, for a photograph of the Maternity Hospital in Loveday Street.

I had never heard of it and thought it might have been a project that was never built. However, it was, and the foundation stone of this building in Loveday Street (later Lower Loveday Street), with a frontage to Princip Street, was laid on Easter Monday 1841 and it opened in 1842, having cost £2,400 to build. Its birth had not been easy, as there had been a 'tumultuous meeting' on the proposed site on 6 August 1840, leading to virulent letters and advertisements in the *Birmingham Journal* with the suggestion that the trouble had been started by followers of the Chartist movement endeavouring to promote their cause, including universal suffrage.

Sadly, the building only survived for a few years fulfilling its original and admirable purpose, the suggestion for its failure being the excessive distance from the town centre. During this time it was used as a place of worship by followers of George Dawson after his secession from Graham Street until the completion of the Church of the Saviour. It does not surprise me that in discussions concerning the obtaining of designs for the building the name of Mr Hansom was mentioned. For most of its existence the building was used as a manufactory or warehouse and known as the 'People's Hall Works'.

Licensed Victuallers' Asylum, 190–4 Bristol Street.

Licensed Victuallers' Asylum. At the anniversary dinner of the Licensed Victuallers' Society in 1845, it was resolved that an asylum should be founded for the decayed members of the trade and their widows.

Land was bought for the sum of £1,118 3*s* and the foundation stone of the asylum building was laid on the 30 August 1848 by Mr Phillips who proposed the scheme when he was mayor. The building, shown on the left in the photograph immediately before St Luke's Church, was designed by D.R. Hill and was built in red bricks with stone dressings and the first inmates were admitted in 1849.

A more suitable description of the facilities would have been almshouses and this description, but not title, was used later. The residents were evacuated in the Second World War and never returned. After the war, the front of the building was removed and the site became a motor car showroom, a use that continued until the mid-1960s.

The General Institution for the Blind, which had existed privately since 1816, became a public institution on 24 April 1848 and occupied premises at 113 Broad Street, but not for long. A new building, in the Jacobean style, designed by Samuel Hemming, was erected in Carpenter Road, the foundation stone was laid on 23 April 1851 and the premises opened on 22 July 1852 having cost over £12,000 to build. The institution gave educational training to many and provided residential accommodation where needed and the name changed to the Birmingham Royal Institution not long before the outbreak of the First World War. Later, a site was acquired in Harborne and Lickey Grange, the former home of Lord Austin, was bought. The Carpenter Road premises were taken over by the BBC in 1953, but were demolished after the corporation moved to Pebble Mill in the late 1960s.

General Institution for the Blind, Carpenter Road, Edgbaston.

Deaf & Dumb Institution, Edgbaston. A meeting was held at St Philip's rectory on 30 November 1812, when it was proposed to open an institution for the deaf and dumb and this was followed by a public meeting at the Blue Coat School which led to the opening of a school. A permanent site was found quickly in Church Road, Edgbaston and the first twenty children were admitted in 1815, although the building was able to accommodate many more. A master's house, designed by Thomas Rickman, was added in 1829 and the original building was replaced by what became the main building, designed by F.W. Fiddian and shown on the photograph, in 1859. Both of these buildings were demolished in 1960.

Deaf & Dumb Institution, Church Road, Edgbaston.

F.B. Osborn carried out several building projects at the end of the nineteenth century and the beginning of the new century. Name changes took place during its history, becoming the Royal Institution for Deaf & Dumb Children early in the twentieth century and followed later by the Royal School for Deaf Children, a name it retained until its closure in 1984.

Kings Heath Institute was built in 1878 and was situated on the corner of Institute Road, the opposite corner being taken up by Kings Heath Board School, built at about the same time. The land was given by J.H. Nettlefold and he was joined in contributing to the cost of the building by the Cartlands and Isaac Bate. The facilities included a library, lecture hall and newsroom, and was the centre of social life for local working class residents for many years.

Kings Heath Institute, High Street, Kings Heath, 1907.

The Working Men's Institute met in the basement from 1882 until the Institute closed in 1933 and then lasted for only another two years. There was also a Kings Heath Institute School on the site before the First World War, but I know nothing of its status. The institute closed in 1933 and F.W. Woolworth took over the building and opened a store, utilising the main hall and basement, which continued until the building was demolished forty years later.

The Edgbaston Assembly Rooms, situated on the corner of Francis Road, were designed by F.B. Osborn in 1882. The building was used for meetings, plays, concerts, dances and receptions and, from 1937, was used by the Warwickshire Masonic Temple. It was demolished in the late 1960s, when the Five Ways area was redeveloped.

Edgbaston Assembly Rooms, Hagley Road.

Kyrle Hall, Sheep Street, Gosta Green.

Kyrle Hall. The Birmingham Kyrle Society was founded in 1880, with the object of bringing natural and artistic beauty into the lives of the citizens of Birmingham. The foundation stone of Kyrle Hall was laid on 22 October 1892 and the building was opened on 28 September 1893, having been designed by W.H. Bidlake.

The Birmingham Guild of Handicraft came into being through the efforts of the Society and it was housed in purpose built workshops at Kyrle Hall and, for a time, Bidlake was the Hon. Director of the Guild. The building was used, also, by the Birmingham Boys' and Girls' Union. Kyrle Hall was rebuilt in 1936 and demolished in 1968, when the land was needed for the expansion of Aston University.

The building at **95 The Parade** was designed by Crouch, Butler & Savage in 1907, for James Speight, who was a photographer. I have chosen it not only because it was an attractive building, but for the better reason that I knew the client. I met him as fellow members of the Sutton Coldfield Civic Society and the Rotary Club of Sutton Coldfield and can remember him giving a talk to the Rotary Club members, the contents of which I cannot remember, but the title was 'Sutton Coldfield in 1902'. The building was later used as showrooms by the Midland Electricity Board and then by Book Sale in the early 1990s, before being demolished later in the decade. Jim Speight died on 9 February 1977 aged ninety-seven.

95 The Parade,
Sutton Coldfield.
*(Supplied by Sutton
Coldfield Reference
Library)*

Bibliography

Bartlam, Norman, *Ladywood in Old Photographs*, Sutton Publishing,1999

Baxter, Marian, *Sutton Coldfield*, Alan Sutton, 1994

—— & Drake, Peter, *Erdington*, Chalford Publishing, 1995

—— & Field, John, *Then and No: Sutton Coldfield* Tempus Publishing, 2002

Chinn, Carl, *The Cadbury Story*, Brewin Books, 1998

Clegg, Chris & Rosemary, *The Dream Palaces of Birmingham* C. & R. Clegg, 1983

Crawford, Alan & Thorne, Robert, *Birmingham Pubs 1890–1939*, University of Birmingham, 1975

Dent, Robert K., *Old and New Birmingham*, Houghton & Hammond, 1880, republished E.P. Publishing, 1973

——, *Making of Birmingham*, J.L. Allday, 1894

Drake, Peter, *Winson Green and Brookfield* Tempus Publishing, 2003

Foster, Andy, *Birmingham*, Yale University Press, 2005

Gill, Conrad, *History of Birmingham to 1865*, Oxford University Press, 1952

Green, Margaret D., *Kings Heath* Tempus Publishing, 1998

Hampson, Martin, *Edgbaston*, Tempus Publishing, 1999

Harrison, Derek, *Birmingham Snow Hill – A First Class Return*, Peter Watts Publishing, 1986

Inglis, Simon, *Villa Park 100 Years*, Sports Projects, 1997

Jones, Douglas V., *The Royal Town of Sutton Coldfield*, Westwood Press, 1979

Langford, John A., *A Century of Birmingham Life from 1741 to 1841*, E.C. Osborne and Simpkin, Marshall & Co., 1868

McKenna, Joseph, *Birmingham as it was the City 1857–1914*, Birmingham Public Libraries, 1979

——, *Birmingham between the Wars*, Birmingham Library Services and Hendon Publishing, 1991

——, *Central Birmingham Pubs*, Tempus Publishing, 2006

Maxam, Andrew, *'Time, Please!'*, Crown Cards, 2002

Price, Victor J., *Birmingham Cinemas*, KAF Brewin Books, 1986

——, *Birmingham Theatres, Concert and Music Halls*, Brewin Books, 1988

Ryerson, Barry, *The Giants of Small Heath: The History of BSA*, Haynes Publishing Group, 1980

Shill, Ray, *Birmingham's Industrial Heritage: 1900–2000*, Sutton Publishing, 2002

——, *Workshop of the World: Birmingham's Industrial Heritage*, Sutton Publishing, 2006

Skipp, Victor, *A History of Greater Birmingham down to 1830*, Victor Skipp, 1980
——, *The Making of Victorian Birmingham* Victor Skipp, 1983
Stephens, W.B.(ed), *A History of the County of Warwick, Volume VII,*
The City of Birmingham Oxford University Press, 1964
Turner, Keith, *Central Birmingham 1870–1920*, Alan Sutton, 1994
——, *Birmingham Pubs*, Tempus Publishing, 1999
Twist, Maria, *Aston and Perry Barr*, Tempus Publishing, 1999
——, *Saltley, Duddeston and Nechells*, Tempus Publishing, 2001
Upton, Chris, *A History of Birmingham*, Phillimore, 1993
Waterhouse, Rachel, *King Edward VI High School for Girls 1883–1983*
Whybrow, John, *How does your Birmingham grow?*, John Whybrow, 1972
——, *How Birmingham became a Great City*, John Whybrow, 1976

I have also consulted:

Kelly's Directories, Wrightson's Directories and Birmingham Reformatory Institution
Annual Reports.

Index of Buildings